The
Conure

An Owner's Guide To

A HAPPY HEALTHY PET

Howell Book House

Howell Book House
A Simon & Schuster Macmillan Company
1633 Broadway
New York, NY 10019

Macmillan Publishing books may be purchased for business or sales promotional use. For information please write: Special Markets Department, Macmillan Publishing USA, 1633 Broadway, New York, NY 10019.

Library of Congress Cataloging-in-Publication Data
Rach, Julie.
The conure: an owner's guide to a happy, healthy pet / Julie Rach.
   p. cm.
ISBN 0-87605226-X

1. Conures.   I. Title.   II. Series.
SF473.C65R335   1998
636.6'865—dc21   98-6585
                        CIP

Manufactured in the United States of America
10 9 8 7 6 5 4 3 2 1

Series Director: Amanda Pisani
Series Assistant Director: Jennifer Liberts
Book Design by Michele Laseau
Cover Design by Iris Jeromnimon
Photography:
   Front and back covers by Eric Ilasenko
   Font cover inset by B. Everett Webb
   Joan Balzarini: 24, 30, 31, 47, 75, 77, 80, 111, 116, 119
   Michael DeFreitas: 40
   Eric Ilasenko: i, 2–3, 8, 13, 23, 25, 26, 27, 33, 36, 38–39, 46, 61, 70, 79, 84, 86, 90, 108, 122
   Kelli Cates: 105
   Sherry Lee Harris: 6, 14, 15, 16, 17, 19, 21, 29, 37, 42, 44, 48, 53, 57, 60, 64, 66, 69, 109, 113, 114
   David Shulman: 81
   John Tyson: 10, 18, 22, 50, 56, 73, 78, 118
   B. Everett Webb: 5, 7, 9, 12, 14, 17, 20, 21, 41, 43, 45, 51, 52, 58, 62, 63, 65, 68, 71, 72, 83, 87, 106–107, 110
Production Team: Clint Lahnen, Stepahnie Mohler, Angel Perez, Heather Pope, Dennis Sheehan, Terri Sheehan

Welcome
to the World

Contents

of the
Conure

External Features of the Conure

Nare

Crown

Cere

Nape

Beak

Mantle

Breast

Rump

Tail Feathers
(Retrices)

chapter 1

About Conures

Conures are New World parrots that were first found throughout Latin America, from Mexico through the islands of the Caribbean to southern Chile. The largest conure is the Patagonian conure, which measures about 17.5 inches long, while the smallest is the Painted conure, which measures 8.5 inches long from the top of her head to the tip of her tail.

The Conure's Background

Conures' native environments include a wide variety of climates and terrains, from savannahs to tropical forests and cooler mountain areas. They are peaceful birds that live in large flocks. Their common name comes from *Conurus*, which is a name that was formerly applied to the genus *Aratinga*. Conures' nesting sites in the wild range from niches carved into sandstone cliffs to tree cavities.

*Conures have
peaceful tempera-
ments and thrive
in large flocks.*

Some species, such as the Red throat, Olive throat, Cuban and Peach front, nest in active termite mounds or termite nests in trees. To do this, the birds break into the termite mound with their beaks and dig a tunnel

WHAT'S IN A NAME?

The conure's common name comes from *Conorus*, which is a name that was formerly applied to the genus *Aratinga*. The genus name is a part of the scientific name, which will appear with more detailed discussions of each species. The scientific name is important because the common name for an animal can vary from country to country and even within a country, causing a great deal of confusion. When the scientific name is used, this confusion is avoided.

Common names are often based on a bird's coloration, who discovered or was somehow connected with the discovery of the bird or where the bird comes from in the wild.

and a nesting chamber. This effort takes them about a week, after which they leave the nest alone for a week so the termites can seal off the nest from the mound. The birds then return and set up housekeeping.

In the wild, conures eat a variety of foods, including grass seeds, fruits, cactus, berries, nuts, flowers, insects and grains. They can also do damage to cultivated crops, which makes them unpopular with farmers in their native habitats.

In southern California, bird watchers may find themselves being entertained by a feral flock of conures (Cherry-heads, Mitreds and Nandays are the most commonly seen species), Amazons and other psittacine species. Bird lovers from the Pacific Palisades to Pasadena have been delighted by the antics of these feral birds that regularly perform gymnastic routines on power lines or raid nut trees. They stay in an area for a few days, then move over a few city blocks to start the routine over again. Another flock has been reported on Telegraph Hill in San Francisco, and other flocks of feral conures have been sighted in Texas, Florida and other temperate climate zones.

THE FIRST DOCUMENTED CONURES

Conures were first described in literature in 1724 by Fr. Labat, who described and drew a species called *Aratinga labati* on the island of Guadaloupe. Some naturalists believe that this green parrot with a few red head feathers may have been a captive Cuban conure (*Aratinga euops*), or she may be a now-extinct species.

Many bird watchers enjoy the antics of feral conures.

The importation of conures into Europe and the United States began over 100 years ago, and a few species, such as the Green conure, were being bred in the United States in the mid-1930s. Unfortunately, at the time, most people believed it was easier to go into the jungle and capture more birds, rather than setting up the birds they had in breeding colonies. With habitat destruction and the increased demand for birds in the pet trade, this situation had to change.

BREEDING CONURES BEGINS

The brightly colored Sun and Jenday conures spurred aviculturists into breeding conures on a large scale. The Sun conure was first imported into the United States in the 1960s, and she was routinely bred in captivity by the 1980s. The Jenday conure soon followed. After that, aviculturists turned their attention to other conure species, which turned out to be a benefit for both pet owners and wild conures. Pet owners received more suitable companion birds when domestic-bred conures were available to the pet trade, and wild conures were less threatened with trapping and exportation because the demand for them decreased.

The Sun conure was first imported into the U.S. in the 1960s.

Although wild-caught birds were still fairly common pets into the early 1980s, most conures offered for sale as pets were domestically bred birds. This means that they were healthier and better suited emotionally to be pets than the wild-caught birds of fifteen or twenty years ago.

Conure Species

Depending on which expert you consult, between 45 and 100 different species and subspecies of birds in six genera make up the group of parrots we call conures. The following discussion does not include all of the different species because not all are commonly kept in the pet trade.

PARROT PARTICULARS

The conure shares certain traits with the Yellow-fronted Amazon and the lovebird because they are all members of parrot species. Characteristics that all parrot species have in common include:

- four toes—two pointing backward and two pointing forward

- upper beak hanging over the lower

- broad head and short neck

For an in-depth look at the different species of conures, consult Joseph Forshaw's *Parrots of the World*, which describes the appearance, native habitat and natural history of each species in detail.

This book will focus primarily on the *Aratinga* (pronounced "ah-rahting-ah") and *Pyrrhura* (pronounced "py-hurrah") genera, which include the most common pet members. Other genera, such as *Nandayus*, *Cyanoliseus* and *Enicognathus*, which have one or two pet-suitable species in them, will also be discussed.

Some breeders think that conures and macaws are closely related. In fact, the genus name *Aratinga* means "little macaw." There are some physical similarities worth noting: similar body shapes, brightly colored feathers and long tails. Further genetic analysis is needed to determine just how close the relationship is that exists between these groups of birds.

One way to distinguish the two genera of conures is to remember that *Aratinga* birds are brightly colored (vibrant greens and reds, for example), while *Pyrrhura* birds are darker in coloration (deep green or maroon). *Aratinga* birds also lack the light-colored markings on the upper chest that *Pyrrhura* birds characteristically have.

The conure has been compared to the macaw due to her body shape, brightly colored feathers and long tail.

chapter 2

All **Types**
of
Conures

In the descriptions that follow, there are scientific names provided to help you distinguish between the species as you read more about conures. Some books classify them by their common names in North America, while others call them by their common British names. The scientific names will assist you in determining which conure is which.

Here, in alphabetical order, are twenty-five conures you may encounter in pet stores, at bird marts or in your visits to bird breeders. Hopefully one of them will prove to be the perfect pet for you!

Austral Conure

(ENICOGNATHUS FERRUGINEUS)

In his native habitat of southern Chile, the Austral conure has the distinction of being the southernmost parrot found in the wild. He measures 14.5 inches in length and weighs about 5 ounces.

In captivity, these drab olive birds with black beaks, gray feet and blackish-gray eye rings make quite good pets. They are less noisy than most conures but they tend to vocalize in the evening. Australs have been exported to Europe and the United States for more than 100 years, but they failed to catch on with breeders because of their dull appearance, so they may be difficult to find.

Australs like to forage on the floor of their cage or aviary, looking for tubers, nuts, seeds, berries and leaf buds. Although bird owners should be concerned if they see their birds on the bottom of their cages all the time, for an Austral conure this is perfectly normal behavior and no cause for alarm. Austral owners do need to pay extra attention to the cleanliness of their pets' cage floors, however, because their birds will be spending more time down there than other species might.

Aztec Conure

(ARATINGA NANA ASTEC)

This conure, which many consider to be a subspecies of the Olive-throated conure, has green head feathers and olive-toned body feathers. His beak is horn-colored and his feet are gray. Aztecs measure about 10 inches in length and weigh about 3 ounces. Their native range is from central Mexico to western Panama.

As pets, Aztecs are known for their talking ability, which is considered quite good for a conure. They are feisty little birds that tend to charm everyone they meet. Somewhat rare as pets, they are worth the wait if you are looking for a small bird with a big personality.

Black-capped Conure
(*Pyrrhura rupicola*)

These uncommon conures have black foreheads, dark-brown chest feathers that are scalloped in off-white, green belly feathers and red feathers on the leading edges of their wings. Their beaks are gray and their legs are dark gray. The Black-cap measures about 10 inches long and weighs about 3 ounces.

Black-caps were imported into the United States from southeastern Peru, northern Bolivia and northwestern Brazil in extremely small numbers about fifteen years ago. However, the small number of birds that came to this country bred prolifically, so this small conure is now available to the pet trade.

Blue-crowned Conure
(*Aratinga acuticaudata*)

Blue-crowned conure.

As his name suggests, the Blue-crown has blue head and facial feathers. The blue coloring becomes more intense as the bird matures. His body feathers are primarily green, the undersides of his wings are yellowish-green and his tail feathers have reddish undersides. These birds have horn-colored beaks, white eye rings that are featherless and pinkish feet.

Blue-crowns measure about 14.5 inches in length and weigh about 7 ounces. Blue-crowns were first bred in captivity in Great Britain in the early 1970s. In the wild, they are found in South America, from Venezuela to Argentina.

Blue-crowns, which are sometimes called Sharp-tailed conures, can be noisy (especially if they are surprised or excited), but they are reasonably peaceful birds.

They have the ability to talk and have friendly personalities.

Brown-throated Conure
(ARATINGA PERTINAX)

This little conure has an orangish face, green wing
and body feathers, buff-colored eye rings, a black
beak and gray legs. He measures about 9.5 inches long
and weighs about 4 ounces. He was imported into
St. Thomas in the Virgin Islands about 125 years ago
and is sometimes called the St. Thomas conure. He is
also found in Central and South America from Panama
to Brazil. There are fourteen recognized subspecies
of this conure, which may also be called the Orange-
cheek or the Brown-ear.

Some conure fanciers believe Brown-throats make
great pets, while others are quick to point out that
these birds can be aggressive, destructive and noisy. As
with all creatures, each Brown-throat has his own personality. In order to determine if he's the right bird for
you, spend some time with a Brown-throated conure
before making a decision to own one.

*A Brown-throated
conure and a
Cherry-headed
conure.*

Cactus Conure
(ARATINGA CACTORUM)

These conures from northeastern Brazil have gray
forehead and throat feathers, a yellowish belly and

13

green wings. Their beaks are horn colored, their eye rings are white and their feet are black. Cactus conures measure about 10 inches in length and weigh about 3 ounces. The bird's common name comes from the fact that cactus fruit comprises a large part of his diet.

Cactus conures can become affectionate pets. They tame readily, are not destructive and tend to be a quieter conure. Unfortunately, Brazil has not exported birds recently, so these little charmers are uncommon as pets, although some breeders are starting to raise them in captivity.

Cactus conure.

Cherry-headed Conure
(*ARATINGA ERYTHROGENYS*)

Sometimes called the Red-headed or Red-masked conure, mature Cherry-heads have red facial feathers; green body feathers with a sprinkling of red on the throat, shoulders and thighs; bare white eye rings; horn-colored beaks and dark gray legs. Mature Cherry-heads are about 13 inches long and weigh between 5 and 7 ounces. Cherry-heads can learn to talk and if they do, they are often fairly quiet birds, opting to speak their owners' language instead of vocalizing in conure speech.

Cherry-headed conure.

Young Cherry-heads are predominantly green until their first molts, and older birds can take up to ten years to fully develop their red plumage. In the wild, Cherry-heads are found in a narrow range in western Ecuador and Peru.

Dusky Conure
(*ARATINGA WEDDELLI*)

Sweetness seems to be a hallmark of this small conure, which is sometimes called Weddell's conure. Other adjectives used to describe him include calm, gentle and mellow. He is not an eye-catching bird, being mostly green with a gray-blue head, white eye rings and a black beak and feet, but his affectionate personality soon wins the heart of his owner. Conure fanciers routinely describe him as quiet, which is not an adjective often used to describe a conure. A Dusky conure can also learn to talk, which may win him even more fans.

Dusky conures.

Duskies measure about 11 inches in length and weigh about 4 ounces. In the wild, they are found from southeastern Colombia to western Brazil.

Finsch's Conure

(*ARATINGA FINSCHI*)

These birds bear a striking resemblance to the Red-fronted, or Wagler's, conure, but Finsch's conures have red feathers on the front edges of their wings. Their body feathers are mostly green, their beaks are horn-colored, their eye rings are creamy white and they have gray-brown legs and feet. Mature Finsch's conures measure about 11 inches in length and weigh about 6 ounces.

As with the Cherry-heads discussed earlier, young Finsch's conures are completely green. As they mature, they develop their characteristic red foreheads. The native range for the Finsch's conure is southern Nicaragua to western Panama.

Gold-capped Conure
(*ARATINGA AURICAPILLA*)

This popular conure has a golden-orange forehead, a green chest and a reddish belly. His eye rings are

white, his beak is gray-black and his legs are gray. The Gold-cap measures about 12 inches in length and weighs about 5 ounces. He is a common cage and aviary bird in the United States.

Gold-caps, sometimes called Golden-headed conures, are prone to lying on their backs in their food bowls or in their owners' hands—it's simply a comfortable position for them. They are active, energetic little birds that have been captive bred in the United States for the past fifteen years. Although they are not as flashy as the yellow-

*Gold-capped
conure.*

orange Jenday or Sun conure, some conure experts believe the Gold-cap makes the least amount of noise and has the best pet potential of this golden trio.

Because his rain-forest habitat is decreasing, the Gold-cap is rare in his native range, which is southeastern Brazil.

Green-cheeked Conure
(*PYRRHURA MOLLINAE*)

Sometimes the Green-cheeked and the Maroon-bellied conure are confused with each other. Although recent chromosomal analysis and DNA fingerprint investigations indicate that they may in fact be the same species, I will nonetheless treat them separately. The Green-cheeked conure and the Maroon-bellied do resemble each other quite closely: Both birds have brown heads, green cheek feathers, brown chest feathers scalloped with buff or yellow, maroon belly and tail feathers, white eye rings, gray beaks and dark-gray legs, but the Green-cheeked has a darker-brown head, less maroon on his belly, more green on his cheeks and a lighter background on the barred area on the chest feathers.

Green-cheeked conure.

The Green-cheeked also has a completely maroon tail.

In the wild, the Green-cheeked is found in west-central Brazil, northern Bolivia and northwestern Argentina. He measures about 10 inches in length and weighs about 4 ounces. Green cheeks make engaging, bold and inquisitive pets. They lack the loud voice of an *Aratinga*, so their vocalizations should be tolerable for most owners.

Half moon Conure
(*ARATINGA CANICULARIS*)

The Half moon, or Petz's conure, is often confused with the Peach-fronted conure. Half moon conures have orange foreheads, olive chest feathers, green wing and belly feathers, horn-colored beaks (as opposed to the Peach front's black beak), orange-yellow eye rings (the Peach front's eye ring has small orange feathers on it) and dark gray feet. Half moons measure 9.5 inches in length and weigh about 2.5 ounces.

Half moon conure.

The Half moon conure may be the best known of the *Aratinga* species because he was widely imported from western Central America for a number of years. Since the 1970s, Half moons have been set up for captive breeding in the United States, and they have produced regularly. Young Half moons are as bold as brass. These fearless

17

birds can learn to talk, and they make tame, affection-ate pets.

Jenday Conure
(ARATINGA JANDAYA)

Jenday conure.

Almost as colorful as the Sun conure, the Jenday is an eye-catching bird that has predominantly orange-red body feathers, green wings with blue accent feathers, white eye rings, a black beak and black-ish feet. Jendays measure about 12 inches in length and weigh about 5 ounces.

This native of northeastern Brazil has not been imported into the United States for about fifteen years. Bird breeders have been able to fill the needs of pet own-ers from domestically bred stock. Although they can be somewhat noisy, Jendays make inquisitive, ac-robatic pets.

Maroon-bellied Conure
(PYRRHURA FRONTALIS)

Like his relative the Green-cheeked, the Maroon-bellied has a brown head, green cheek feathers, brown chest feathers scalloped with buff or yellow, a ma-roon belly and tail feathers, white eye rings, a gray beak and dark-gray legs. In contrast to the Green-cheeked, the Maroon-bellied, as his name suggests, has a larger patch of maroon belly feathers, more yel-low on his chest and green head feathers. Maroon-bellieds measure about 10 inches in length and weigh about 3 ounces.

Maroon-bellieds, which may also be called Scaly-breasted conures, were imported into the United States and Europe from their native ranges in south-eastern Brazil, Uruguay, Paraguay and northern

Argentina since the 1920s. The species has since been set up in captive-breeding situations, in which pairs have produced chicks quite well. Maroon-bellieds have large personalities in their small bodies, and they make lively, playful pets.

Maroon-bellied conures.

Maroon-tailed Conure
(PYRRHURA MELANURA)

This conure also goes by the name of the Black-tailed conure. He measures about 9.5 inches in length and weighs about 3 ounces. The Maroon-tailed has a brown forehead; green cheeks, wings and belly feathers and brown-green chest feathers that are scalloped with white. The Maroon-tailed also has red feathers on the leading edge of his wings. His eye rings are white, while his beak and feet are gray. As you might expect, his tail feathers are black on top and maroon on the underside, which gives rise to both of his common names.

In the wild, Maroon-tailed conures are found from southern Venezuela to northeastern Peru. Maroon-taileds make entertaining pets. They enjoy being around people and take to strangers rather quickly, winning new friends with their charming personalities.

Mitred Conure
(ARATINGA MITRATA)

Mitred conures are primarily green birds with reddish foreheads, creamy-white eye rings, horn-colored beaks

19

and brown legs. As with other green-and-red conures discussed here, young Mitreds are completely green until their first molts, when their red foreheads start to become evident. Mitreds measure 15 inches in length and weigh about 8.5 ounces.

Mitreds became well known to pet owners at the height of importation, when thousands of these parrots were

Mitred conures.

brought into the United States from the Mitred's native habitat, which stretches from central Peru to northwestern Argentina. Their popularity is even greater with the introduction of domestically bred birds into the pet trade.

Although Mitreds can be quite vocal, they are also quite affectionate pets. This loyal affection for their owners has won this species many fans over the years. They are also prone to chew, so be sure to provide your Mitred with lots of toys he can destroy.

Nanday Conure
(*NANDAYUS NENDAY*)

One of the more colorful conure species, the Nanday has a black forehead and cheeks, a bluish throat, green belly and wing feathers, orange leg feathers, white eye rings, a black beak and pink feet. Nandays, which are also known as Black-headed or Black-masked conures, measure 12 inches in length and weigh about 5 ounces.

Nandays have been exported from their native habitat, which ranges from southeastern Bolivia to northern Argentina, for more than 100 years. As is the case with many wild-caught parrots, wild-caught Nandays developed a reputation as poor-quality pets. Today's hand-fed, domestically bred pet Nandays, on the other hand, are difficult to beat. They are naturally social birds that thrive on attention from their owners, and they get along well with other parrots. The Nanday's main drawback as a pet is that some of them can be quite loud, so they may not be well suited for life in an apartment or town house.

Nanday conure.

It's difficult to be indifferent about a Nanday because these acrobatic little extroverts quickly charm their way into your heart. Many Nanday owners are extremely loyal to their colorful little friends. First-time owners need to remember that Nandays are prone to falling asleep on their backs with their feet in the air, a behavior which can be alarming the first time you see it.

Patagonian conure.

Patagonian Conure
(*CYANOLISEUS PATAGONUS*)

This is the largest conure, measuring about 17.5 inches in length and weighing a little more than ½ pound. Although some might describe their plumage as dull, Patis are actually quite colorful with their olive heads, orange and yellow bellies, blue flight feathers, pink feet, black beaks and white eye rings. The natural range for this conure is central Chile, northern and central Argentina and southern Uruguay.

In the wild, Patis are known to be ground feeders, so don't be alarmed if your Pati spends an unusual amount of time on the bottom of his cage. As long as the bird appears otherwise healthy, this is a natural behavior. Patis are quite cuddly pets, and some can become good talkers. Among the drawbacks to keeping these conures are the facts that they can be quite loud, they require large cages to be comfortable and they are voracious chewers.

Peach-fronted Conure
(ARATINGA AUREA)

*Peach-fronted
conure.*

Sometimes called the Golden-crowned conure, the Peach-fronted conure can be easily confused with the

Half moon described above. Peach-fronts have deep-orange foreheads, olive throats, yellow belly feathers and green wing feathers. Their beaks and feet are black, and their eye rings are covered with small orange feathers.

The Peach-fronted occupies a wide range—southern Brazil to northern Argentina—in his native habitat. He measures about 10 inches in length and weighs about 4 ounces.

Peach-fronted conures have been kept by bird owners and breeders for more than 100 years. As pets, these conures have fairly good talking abilities and sweet dispositions. However, they can be destructive, noisy and aggressive toward other parrots during the breeding season.

Queen of Bavaria Conure

(*ARATINGA GUAROUBA*)

The Queen of Bavaria is a large, visually striking bird. His primary feather color is brilliant yellow with olive green flight feathers, and he has a horn-colored beak, white eye rings and pinkish feet. Queens measure about 14 inches in length and weigh about ½ pound. Because they are so eye-catching, they have been featured in advertisements for premium bird foods in some of the bird specialty magazines. The San Diego Zoo has a pair of Queens on display that I make a point of visiting each time I'm at the zoo. These large conures cause more than a few visitors to stop and take a second look.

Queen of Bavaria conure.

Queens, which are sometimes referred to as Golden conures, are native to a small area in northeastern Brazil. They are endangered in the wild because of deforestation, nest site destruction and human colonization. They have a long history of captive breeding that dates from Sri Lanka in 1939. This species has been bred in the United States for more than 50 years. Despite this long history in captivity, Queens are uncommon pets and they command top dollar in the market.

Queens are prone to a few behavioral problems, including loud vocalization, feather picking and aggression toward other parrots, particularly during breeding season. However, they are generally tame and affectionate toward their owners. This species is not recommended for first-time conure owners because they require great deal of attention and because they are still uncommonly kept in aviculture.

Red-fronted Conure
(ARATINGA WAGLERI)

Also known as Wagler's conure, the Red-fronted is a green bird with a red forehead, white eye rings, a horn-colored beak and brownish feet. Young birds start out life completely green and develop their red foreheads as they mature. The Red-fronted measures about 14.5 inches in length and weighs about 6.5 ounces.

*Red-fronted
conure.*

In the wild, the Red-fronted conure's native range stretches in a narrow band from northern Venezuela to southern Peru. These birds have been bred in captivity in the United States since 1957. They make entertaining pets and are capable of learning a variety of tricks.

Red-throated Conure
(ARATINGA HOLOCHLORA RUBRITORQUIS)

This subspecies of the green conure makes a comical pet that has a good chance of becoming a talking bird. Red-throated conures measure about 12 inches in length and weigh about 4 ounces.

In the wild, Red-throateds are found from eastern Guatemala to northern Nicaragua. Across their range, these birds are highly prized as pets. They were not imported to the United States in large numbers, but the birds that are here have bred well in captivity.

Like some other types of conures, young Red-throateds start out life as all-green birds (well, once they have their feathers, anyway). They develop their red throats after their first molts. Red-throats also have beige eye rings, horn-colored beaks and brownish legs.

Slender-billed Conure
(ENICOGNATHUS LEPTORHYNCHUS)

Like the Austral, this drab olive conure with gray eye rings, a reddish stripe of feathers around his eyes, a black beak and grayish feet has been largely over-

Slender-billed conure.

looked in the pet trade because he simply doesn't have eye-catching plumage. He does, however, have an eye-catching beak that may cause some first-time bird owners to think something is wrong with the bird. His upper mandible is considerably longer than those of other parrots, but it's simply an adaptation that allows the Slender-billed to dig for tubers and roots in his native habitat of central Chile. The elongated bill also helps the bird retrieve one of his favorite foods—the seeds of the *Araucaria araucana* tree. Slender-billed conures kept in captivity may appreciate pine nuts, which are similar to their favorite wild seeds.

Slender-billed conures, which are sometimes called Long-billed conures, are one of the larger conures, measuring about 16 inches in length and weighing about 6 ounces. They are peaceful birds that adapt well to captivity. They can be quite noisy when they want to be, but they can also learn to talk rather well. Slender-billeds are prone to spending long periods of time on the cage floor, foraging for food, so don't be alarmed if your Slender-billed seems to be down in his cage bottom all the time. You can make the hunt for food more interesting for this bird by scattering a few seeds in the bottom of his cage. Be alert to the condition of the cage bottom and keep it scrupulously clean to help ensure the health of your conure.

Sun Conure
(ARATINGA SOLSTITIALIS)

These flashy little birds have been described as the Cadillacs of the conure group. A mature Sun conure is

a brilliant blaze of orange, yellow, red and green feathers, while younger Sun conures have a mottled green plumage until their first molts. Mature Suns have black beaks, white eye rings and grayish feet. They measure about 12 inches in length and weigh about 4.5 ounces.

Suns are found in the wild from Guyana to northeastern Brazil, but they have been captive bred in the United States for many years. As pets, they are known for being content to be with their owners for hours at a time, sit-

Sun conure.

ting on a shoulder or the back of a chair. They can be noisy if ignored, but otherwise make fine pets.

White-eyed Conure
(ARATINGA LEUCOPHTHALMUS)

White-eyed conures take their name from the bare ring of white skin around their eyes. They are predominantly green birds with a sprinkling of red feathers on their bodies, horn-colored beaks and gray-brown legs. White-eyed conures measure about 13 inches in length and weigh about 4.5 ounces.

In the wild, White-eyed conures can be found from Guyana to Uruguay. In captivity, they can be quite affectionate, engaging pets and may learn to talk at a quite early age.

chapter 3

Choosing the Right
Conure
for You

Before you decide to bring a conure into your life, you'll need to
consider a few questions. Do you
like animals? Do you have the time
to care for one properly? Can you
have pets where you live? Can you
live with a little mess (seed hulls,
feathers and discarded food) in
your home? Can you tolerate, and
appreciate, a little noise (the kind
made by an excited conure) as
part of your daily routine?

Why a Bird?

If you've answered "yes" to all of
these questions, you're a good
candidate for bird ownership.
Now you might be wondering:

"Why do I want a bird?" Here are some answers you might come up with:

Birds make good companions. Although a bird isn't quite as loyal as a dog, she isn't as aloof as many cats you'll meet, either. As an added bonus, many birds can learn to whistle or talk, which is beyond the range of canine and feline ability and which many owners find amusing or entertaining.

Birds have a long life span. A cockatoo named King Tut greeted visitors at the San Diego Zoo for seventy years, and *Bird Talk* magazine reported on a documented 106-year-old Amazon in Alaska. Smaller birds can live long lives, too; the *Guinness Book of Records* reports an almost-30-year old Budgerigar in Great Britain.

Birds need consistent, but not constant, attention. This can be a benefit for today's busy single people and families. While birds can't be ignored completely, they are content to entertain themselves for part of the day while their owners are busy elsewhere.

Many of my evenings have been brightened by the presence of my bird, Sindbad. She is content to sit on my lap and have her back rubbed or her head scratched while we watch TV together. She asks for very little except regular feedings and cage cleanings and a bit of attention each day, and she offers companionship and unconditional love in return.

Birds' small sizes make them great pets for today's small living spaces. More of us are living in apartments, mobile or manufactured homes and condominiums, which makes the ownership of large pets that need yards and lots of regular exercise awkward and inconvenient. Birds just seem to fit better in apartments, condos, mobile homes and other smaller living spaces.

Birds are relatively quiet pets. Unless you have a particularly vocal macaw or cockatoo, most birds aren't likely to annoy the neighbors the way a barking dog or a yowling cat can. In many rental situations, birds aren't even considered pets, which means you can keep them without having to surrender a sizable security deposit to your landlord.

Birds may be easier to maintain than dogs and cats. As one who has had all three types of pets, I think that the daily maintenance time a bird requires may be less than what a dog or cat needs. Birds don't have to be walked, they don't require as much grooming as a longhaired dog or cat, nor do they shed as much. And there's only a cage and small bowls to clean, instead of bowls and a litter box for a cat or the whole yard in the case of a dog.

Birds provide a "reason to get up in the morning." This cannot be overestimated for older bird owners and single people who are on their own. Birds provide all the benefits realized in the human/animal bond, such as lower blood pressure and reduced levels of stress in owners who interact regularly with their pets.

Finally, birds are intelligent pets. Whoever coined the phrase "bird-brain" didn't truly appreciate how smart some birds are. Some larger parrots have scored at levels comparable to chimpanzees, dolphins and preschool-age children on intelligence tests.

Are you purchasing a conure on a whim because you're attracted to her beautiful colors? Are you rescuing a bird from her aggressive cagemates? Are you buying a bird you otherwise feel sorry for? Noble though some of these reasons are, none of them is a good reason for purchasing a pet bird. Birds purchased for their pretty colors may soon be ignored or neglected by owners whose attentions have been captured by another fancy, and small, timid birds may be hiding signs of illness that can be difficult and costly to cure and that can cause an owner much heartache in the process.

Birds have smarts; some learn to whistle tunes, some are able to speak and many can learn to perform tricks.

If you feel the urge to become a bird owner, and you've bought this book instead, you're on the right road. If you purchased this book along with your conure, this is also a good first step, or if you've picked up this book after having your bird a few weeks or months, congratulations! You're on the road to responsible bird ownership.

Before you bring your conure home, budget your time to make room in your life for your new pet.

The Bottom Line

Conures are available in many price ranges, from affordable to extravagantly expensive. To help keep you from losing your head and a large portion of your bank account, here are some things you'll want to think about as you become a conure owner:

• the cost of the bird herself

• the cost of her cage and accessories

• the cost of bird food (seeds, formulated diets and fresh foods)

• the cost of toys

• the cost of veterinary care

• the amount of time you can devote to your bird each day

• who will care for the bird if you go on vacation or are called out of town unexpectedly

• how many other pets you already own

• the size of your home

Please read on to learn more about the conure's personality and the background of the bird you've chosen.

Where Will You Get Your Conure?

Conures can be purchased through several sources, including bird breeders, who will advertise in bird specialty magazines, the pet section of your newspaper's classified ads or on the Internet; bird shows and marts, which offer breeders and buyers an opportunity to get together and share their love of birds, and bird specialty stores. Let's look at each in a bit more detail.

Classified advertisements are usually placed by private parties who want to place pets in new homes. If the advertiser offers young birds, you've found a private breeder who wants to place a few birds in good homes. Most pet conures can leave the breeder's home at around 3 months of age. Some breeders may also offer older birds for sale from time to time. These are most likely breeder birds that are too old to produce chicks but that are still good candidates for pet situations.

Bird shows and marts offer bird breeders and bird buyers an opportunity to get together to share a love for birds. Bird shows can provide prospective bird owners with the chance to see many different types of birds all in one place, which can help you narrow your choices if you're undecided about which species to keep. At a bird show, you can watch to see which birds win consistently, then talk to the breeder of these birds after the show to see if he or she expects any chicks.

Buy your conure from a clean, well-kept store that has a knowledgeable and friendly staff.

A bird mart is a little different from a bird show. At a bird mart, various species of birds and a wide variety of bird-keeping supplies are offered for sale, so you can go and shop to your heart's content.

Bird specialty stores may be the ideal place to purchase a conure. If a store in your area sells conures, you'll

31

need to visit the store and make sure it's clean and well kept. Walk around the store a bit. Do the cages look and smell like they're cleaned regularly? Do the birds in the cages appear alert, well fed and healthy? Do the cages appear crowded or do the animals inside have some room to move around?

IS THIS CONURE HEALTHY?

Here are some of the indicators of a healthy conure. Keep them in mind when selecting your pet, and reject any birds that do not meet these criteria.

- bright eyes
- a clean cere (the area above the bird's beak that covers her nares or nostrils)
- an upright posture
- quiet breathing
- a full-chested appearance
- active movement around the cage
- clean legs and vent
- smooth feathers
- a good appetite

Remember that healthy birds spend their time doing four main activities—eating, playing, defecating and sleeping—in about equal amounts of time. If you notice that a bird seems to only want to sleep, for instance, reject that bird in favor of another whose routine seems more balanced.

Look at the birds that are available for sale. If possible, sit down and watch them for awhile. Don't rush this important step. Do some of them seem bolder than the others? Consider those first, because you want a curious, active, robust pet, rather than a shy animal that hides in a corner.

You may think that saving a small, picked-upon conure from her cage-mates seems like the right thing to do, but please resist this urge. You want a strong, healthy, spirited bird rather than "the runt of the litter." Although it sounds hard-hearted, automatically reject any birds that are being bullied, are timid or that hide in a corner or shy away from you. It will save you some heartache in the end.

If possible, let your conure choose you. Many bird stores display their livestock on T-stands or play gyms, or a breeder may bring out a clutch of babies for you to look at. If one bird waddles right up to you and wants to play, or if one comes over to check you out and just seems to want to come home with you, that's the bird you want!

WHAT'S THAT BAND MEAN?

As you select your pet, you may notice leg bands on the birds you're looking at and wonder why the birds are wearing them. Bird bands serve several purposes. First, they help identify a particular breeder's stock. They can also help establish an age for your bird, because many of them have the year of hatch as part of the band's code. Finally, some states require that pet birds be banded with closed, traceable bands so that the origin of the bird can be determined. This type of regulation is an effort to reduce the number of smuggled birds that are kept as pets in the United States.

THE PREOWNED PARROT

As you make your selection of the right conure for you, you may see adult birds advertised for sale at a bird store or in the newspaper. Adopting an adult conure could be a great mistake (if the bird has a number of behavioral problems) or it could be the best investment you'll ever make.

People put adult conures up for sale for many reasons. Perhaps the bird detects stress in the home and begins to pull her feathers, and the owners have neither the time nor the patience to solve the problem. The owners may have a child and suddenly no longer have time for the parrot, or they may be moving and cannot take their pet with them. Some people simply lose interest in their birds and sell them after a few years.

Leg bands on birds help to identify where they came from and how old they are.

If you want to consider a preowned parrot, make an appointment to see the bird in her current home. Ask why the owners are selling the bird and see if you and the bird "click." Sometimes a change of owners is all a bird needs to really become a wonderful pet—for example, my African grey was unhandleable and downright nippy in her previous home, but now she cuddles with me on the couch in the evenings as we watch TV and seems to expect daily handling and petting.

Conure Characteristics

Conures are outgoing, cheerful, inquisitive little acrobats that take an active interest in their surroundings and the activities of their human family. They are also intelligent, playful and extremely affectionate.

Although they are smaller members of the parrot family, conures have large personalities and sometimes seem to be unaware of or unable to remember their size. To prevent tragic consequences and an emergency trip to the veterinary hospital, conure owners should closely supervise interactions with these birds and other pets, such as larger parrots, dogs and cats.

Conures offer something for almost anyone. Some species are known to be cuddly, while others can learn to talk fairly well, and still others are strikingly beautiful. Most are also quite affordable pets.

Another interesting aspect of the conure personality is the tendency to snuggle under something when they sleep. Don't be surprised to find your bird under a corner of her cage paper if the cage she lives in doesn't have a grille to keep the bird out of the cage tray. You can provide your conure with a washcloth, a fuzzy toy or something else cuddly to snuggle with.

Conures also fall asleep in their food bowls, often on their backs with their feet in the air. This seems to be an awkward or uncomfortable position to bird owners, and may cause you to panic. You may fear that she has died the first time you see your bird do this. Despite its alarming first impression, there's nothing wrong with your conure if she naps on her back. Some parent birds even feed their chicks when the chicks are lying

CONURE SLEEPING HABITS

Don't become alarmed the first time you see your conure asleep with her head tucked under her wing and resting on one leg. Although it seems that your bird has lost her head or a leg, it's fine. Sleeping on one foot with her head tucked under her wing (actually with her head turned about 180° and her beak tucked into the feathers on the back of her neck) is a normal sleeping position for many parrots, although it looks a bit unusual or uncomfortable to bird owners. Be aware, too, that your bird will occasionally perch on one leg while resting the other. Remember, some conures routinely sleep on their backs, so don't become alarmed if your bird chooses to do this. As long as she appears healthy, eats well and acts normally, you have no cause for concern if your conure sleeps on her back.

on their backs, so it's a perfectly comfortable position for a conure to be in.

Conures are also great bathers. Be aware of this because they'll try to bathe in their water bowls if nothing else is available, but they really prefer to be dunked under the water faucet or to stand under a light shower in the kitchen sink. Be sure the water is lukewarm before letting your conure take a quick dip, and allow plenty of time for your bird's feathers to dry before she goes to bed (a blow dryer set on low can accelerate the drying process).

Finally, conures can be excellent escape artists, so make sure that the cage you select for your conure is completely secure and that the door and cage grille are not prone to popping open or falling out. Make sure the food and water bowl openings have covers that you can slide into place to help keep your pet in her cage while you're changing the bowls. Check to see that all windows in your home have screens on them and doors to the outside world are closed tightly before you let your conure out of her cage.

> ## ENCOURAGING YOUR CONURE TO TALK
>
> While conures will make noises in their "language," they are not noted talkers. Some will learn a few phrases if the phrases are interesting to them. To improve your chances of having a talking bird, keep the following tips in mind:
>
> - Start with a single phrase and work with it until the bird learns it.
>
> - Speak in a bright, cheerful voice.
>
> - Keep the training sessions short (between ten and fifteen minutes) and repeat them several times a day.
>
> - Maintain a positive attitude and tone when talking to the bird.
>
> - Be patient.
>
> If your bird talks, consider that a bonus. Don't make speaking ability the prime reason to own a parrot because chances are you'll be disappointed and you'll miss out on a wonderful opportunity to have a great pet!

OWNERSHIP CHALLENGES

An awareness of the behavioral quirks of conures will help you better prepare for them and may help you decide whether or not a conure is really the bird for you.

First, conures are noted chewers, which means that they will need to have an abundant supply of toys that can be destroyed. If you don't provide them with proper chewing stimulation, they will find it in other places in your home, such as your entryway banister or houseplants. Be sure to supervise your conure when she is out of her cage to prevent her from chewing on inappropriate and potentially harmful things in your home.

Next, conures can and will vocalize, and many of them can be quite loud when they make themselves heard. Generally, members of the *Aratinga* genus of conures are louder than those of the *Pyrrhura* genus, but that's only a general rule and exceptions to it abound.

Conures are small parrots with lots of personality.

To help ensure that you get a relatively quiet conure, purchase a hand-fed bird that has been properly socialized by the breeder. This means that the breeder paid attention to each and every chick and took the time to handle and play with them.

If your conure seems curious about the world around her and trusting of new people, chances are very good that she was socialized well by her breeder. You will need to continue this process by playing with your parrot and helping her explore her new environment (your home) in a safe, secure way.

Once your conure comes home with you, you should give her regular periods of attention and lots of toys to play with when you aren't around. By doing this, you should be able to minimize any loud vocal outbursts.

Bringing Your Conure Home

Choosing the
Right Conure
for You

Give your conure a chance to adjust to your family's routine gradually after you bring her home. Your new pet will need some time to adjust to her new environment, so be patient. After you set your conure up in her cage for the first time, spend a few minutes talking quietly to your new pet, and use her name frequently while you're talking.

After a couple of days of adjustment, your conure should start to settle into her routine. You will be able to tell when your new pet has adjusted to your home, because healthy and relaxed conures will spend about equal amounts of time during the day eating, playing, sleeping and defecating. By observation, you will soon recognize your pet's normal routine. You may also notice that your bird fluffs or shakes her feathers to greet you, or that she chirps a greeting when you uncover her cage in the morning.

Conures love to chew—be sure to provide your bird with toys for this purpose.

Living
with a

part two

Conure

chapter 4

Conure
Care Tips

Despite what you may think, bird keeping isn't particularly difficult. In fact, if you only do ten things for your conure for as long as you own him, your bird will have a pretty healthy and well-adjusted life.

Ten Steps to Better Bird Care

First, provide a safe, secure cage in a safe, secure location in your home. This cage should have appropriate-sized bar spacing and cage accessories that are designed for conures. It should also be located in a fairly active part of your home (the family room, for example) so your bird will feel as if he's part of your family and your daily routine.

Next, clean the cage regularly to protect your pet from illness and to make his surroundings more enjoyable for both of you. Would you want to live in a smelly, dirty house? Your bird won't like it either.

Third, clip your bird's wings regularly to ensure his safety. Bird-proof your home as well, and practice bird safety by closing windows and doors securely before you let your bird out of his cage, keeping your bird indoors when he isn't caged and ensuring that your pet doesn't chew on anything harmful (from houseplants to leaded glass lampshades to power cords) or become poisoned by toxic fumes from overheated nonstick cookware, cleaning products or other household products.

Fourth, offer your conure a varied diet that includes seeds or pellets, fresh vegetables and fruits cut into conure-sized portions and healthy people food, such as raw or cooked pasta, fresh or toasted whole-wheat bread and unsweetened breakfast cereals.

In addition to giving your conure nutritious foods, don't feed your pet chocolate, alcohol, avocado or highly sugared, salted or fatty foods. Provide the freshest food possible, and remove partially eaten or discarded food from the cage before it has a chance to spoil and make your pet sick. Your conure should also have access to clean, fresh drinking water at all times.

Your conure will be happiest when he is involved in family activity.

Next, establish a good working relationship with a qualified avian veterinarian early on in your bird ownership (preferably on your way home from the pet store or breeder). Don't wait for an emergency to locate a veterinarian.

Sixth, take your conure to the veterinarian for regular checkups, as well as when you notice a change in his routine. Illnesses in birds are sometimes difficult to detect before it's too late to save the bird, and preventive care goes far in maintaining your bird's health.

Seventh, set and maintain a routine for your conure. Make sure he's fed at about the same time each day, his playtime out of his cage occurs regularly and his bedtime is well established.

Eighth, provide an interesting environment for your bird. Make him feel that he's part of your family. Entertain and challenge your bird's curiosity with a variety of safe toys. Rotate these toys in and out of your bird's cage regularly, and discard any that become soiled, broken, frayed, worn or otherwise unsafe.

A varied diet, including fruits and vegetables, will help keep your conure healthy.

Ninth, leave a radio or television on for your bird when you are away from home, because a too-quiet environment can be stressful for many birds, and stress can cause illness or other problems for your pet.

Finally, pay attention to your conure on a consistent basis. Don't lavish abundant attention on the bird when you first bring him home, and then gradually lose interest in him. Birds are sensitive, intelligent creatures that will not understand such a mixed message. Set aside a portion of each day to spend with your conure—you'll both enjoy it and your relationship will benefit from it. Besides, wasn't companionship one of the things you were looking for when you picked your conure as a pet?

Now that doesn't seem too difficult, does it? Just devote a little time each day to your pet bird, and soon the two of you will have formed a lifelong bond of trust and mutual enjoyment.

Conure Care Throughout the Year

Your conure requires a certain level of care each day to ensure his health and well-being. Here are some of the things you'll need to do each day for your pet:

- Observe your pet for any changes in his routine (report any changes to your avian veterinarian immediately).

- Offer your bird fresh food and remove old food. Wash the food dish thoroughly with detergent and water. Rinse thoroughly and allow to dry.

- Check the seed dish and refill as necessary with clean, fresh seed.

- Provide fresh water and remove the previous dish. Wash the dish as above.

- Change the paper in the cage tray.

- Let the bird out of his cage for supervised play-time.

Don't be alarmed if you catch your conure snoozing—he needs about ten to twelve hours of sleep a day.

- Finally, cover your bird's cage at about the same time every night to indicate bedtime. Conures seem to thrive when they have a familiar routine. When you cover the cage, you'll probably hear your bird rustling around for a bit, perhaps getting a drink of water or a last mouthful of seeds before settling in for the night. Keep in mind that your pet will require ten to twelve hours of sleep a day, but you can expect that he will take naps during the day to supplement his nightly snooze.

Monitoring Health

Although it may seem a bit unpleasant to discuss, your bird's droppings require daily monitoring because they can tell you a lot about his general health. Conures produce white-and-green tubular-shaped droppings. These droppings are usually composed of equal amounts of fecal material (the green portion), urine (a clear liquid portion) and urates (the white- or cream-colored part).

Texture and consistency, along with frequency or lack of droppings, can let you know how your pet is feeling. For example, if a bird eats a lot of fruits and vegetables, his droppings are generally looser and more watery than a bird that eats primarily seeds. But watery droppings can also indicate illness, such as diabetes or kidney problems, which cause a bird to drink more water than usual.

The color of droppings is also a good indicator of health concerns. Birds that have psittacosis typically have bright, lime-green droppings, while healthy birds have avocado- or darker-green and white droppings. Birds with liver problems may produce droppings that are yellowish or reddish, while birds that have internal bleeding will produce dark, tarry droppings.

However, a change in the color of droppings doesn't necessar-

Your bird's diet will affect the color and consistency of his droppings.

ily indicate poor health. For instance, birds that eat pelleted diets tend to have darker droppings than their seed-eating companions, while parrots that have splurged on a certain fresh food soon have droppings with that characteristic color. Birds that overindulge on beets, for example, produce bright-red droppings that can look for all the world as though the bird has suffered some serious internal injury. Other birds that overdo sweet potatoes, blueberries or raspberries produce orange, blue or red droppings.

As part of your daily cage cleaning and observation of your feathered friend, look at his droppings carefully. Learn what is normal for your bird in terms of color, consistency and frequency, and report any changes to your avian veterinarian promptly.

WEEKLY CHORES

Some of your weekly chores will include:

* Removing old food from the cage bars and from the corners of the cage where it invariably falls.

* Removing, scraping and replacing the perches to keep them clean and free of debris (you might also want to sand them lightly with coarse-grain sandpaper to clean them further and improve perch traction for your pet).

* Rotating toys in your bird's cage to keep them interesting. Remember to discard any toys that show excessive signs of wear (frayed rope, cracked plastic or well-chewed wood).

CAGE CLEANING

Simplify the weekly cage-cleaning process by placing the cage in the shower and letting hot water from the shower head do some of the work. Be sure to remove your bird, his food and water dishes, the cage tray paper and his toys before putting the cage into the shower. You can let the hot water run over the cage for a few minutes, then scrub at any stuck-on food with an old toothbrush or some fine-grade steel wool. After you've removed the food and other debris, you can disinfect the cage with a spray-on, bird-safe disinfectant.

Regularly examine your bird's toys for sharp edges and other signs of excessive wear.

45

Rinse the cage thoroughly and dry it completely before returning your bird and his accessories to the cage. Dry wooden perches more quickly by placing the wet dowels in a 400° oven for ten minutes. (Let the perches cool before you put them back in the cage.)

WEATHER PRECAUTIONS

Warm weather requires a little extra vigilance on the part of a pet-bird owner to ensure that your pet remains comfortable. To help keep your pet cool, keep

him out of direct sun, offer him lots of fresh, juicy vegetables and fruits (be sure to remove these fresh foods from the cage promptly to prevent your bird from eating spoiled food) and mist him lightly with a clean spray bottle (filled with water only) that is used solely for birdie showers.

Warm weather may also bring out a host of insect pests to bedevil you and your bird. Depending on where you live, you may see ants, mosquitoes or other bugs around your bird's cage as the temperature rises. Take care to keep your bird's cage scrupulously clean to discourage any pests, and remove any fresh foods promptly to keep insects out

Keep your bird out of the direct sun to keep him comfortable when the weather gets warm.

of your bird's food bowl. Finally, in cases of severe infestation, you may have to use Camicide or other bird-safe insecticides to reduce the insect population. (Remove your bird from the area of infestation before spraying.) If the problem becomes severe enough to require professional exterminators, make arrangements to have your bird out of the house for at least twenty-four hours after spraying has taken place.

By the same token, pay attention to your pet's needs when the weather turns cooler. You may want to use a heavier cage cover, especially if you lower the heat in your home at bedtime, or you may want to move the bird's cage to another location in your home that is warmer and less drafty.

Your conure may need you to scratch spots he can't reach while he's molting.

Molting

At least once a year, your conure will lose his feathers. Don't be alarmed—this is a normal process called molting. Many pet birds seem to be in a perpetual molt, with feathers falling out and coming in throughout the summer.

You can consider your bird in molting season when you see many whole feathers in the bottom of the cage and you notice that your bird seems to have broken out in a rash of stubby little aglets (those plastic tips on the ends of your shoelaces). These are the feather sheaths that help new pinfeathers

> ### WARM WEATHER WARNING
>
> On a warm day, you may notice your bird sitting with his wings held away from his body, rolling his tongue and holding his mouth open. This is how a bird cools himself off. Watch your bird carefully on warm days because he can overheat quickly, and may suffer heatstroke, which requires veterinary care. If you live in a warm climate, ask your avian veterinarian how you can protect your bird from this potentially serious problem.

break through the skin, and they are made of keratin (the same material that makes up our fingernails). The sheaths also help protect growing feathers from damage until the feather completes its growth cycle.

You may notice that your conure is a little more irritable during the molt; this is to be expected. Think about how you would feel if you suddenly had all these itchy new feathers coming in. However, your bird may actively seek out more time with you during the molt because owners are handy to have around when a conure has an itch on the top of his head that he can't quite scratch!

Scratch these new feathers gently, because some of them may still be growing in and may be sensitive to the touch. You may want to try rolling the newly forming feathers gently between your fingers to open up the feather sheaths without causing your conure too much discomfort.

Moving with a Conure

If moving is in your future, your first step should be to acclimate your bird to traveling in the car. Some pet birds take to this new adventure immediately, while others become so stressed out by the trip that they become car-sick. Patience and persistence are usually the keys to success if your pet falls into the latter category.

If car travel distresses your bird, try taking small trips to help him get the hang of it.

To get your conure used to riding in the car, start by taking his cage (with door and cage tray well secured) out to your car and placing it inside. Make sure that your car is cool before you do this, because your conure can suffer heatstroke if you place him in a hot car and leave him there.

When your bird seems comfortable sitting in his cage in your car, place the cage in the back seat, secure it with a seat belt and take your pet for a short drive, such as around the block. If your bird seems to enjoy the ride (he eats, sings, whistles, talks and generally acts like nothing is wrong), then you have a willing traveler on your hands. If he seems distressed by the ride (he sits on the floor of his cage shaking, screams or vomits), then you have a bit of work ahead.

Distressed birds often need only to be conditioned that car travel can be fun. You can do this by talking to your bird throughout the trip. Praise him for good behavior and reassure him that everything will be fine. Offer special treats and juicy fruits (grapes, apples or citrus fruit) so that your pet will eat and will also take in water.

As your bird becomes accustomed to car travel, gradually increase the length of the trips. When your bird is comfortable with car rides, begin to condition him for the move by packing your car as you would on moving day. If, for example, you plan to place duffel bags near your bird's cage, put the bags and the cage in the back of the car for a "practice run" before you actually begin the move so your bird can adjust to the size, shape and color of the bags. A little planning on your part will result in a well-adjusted avian traveler and a reduced stress level for you both.

Before you move, make a final appointment with your bird's veterinarian. Have the bird evaluated, and ask for a health certificate (this may come in handy when crossing state lines). Also ask for a copy of your conure's records that you can take with you, or arrange to have a copy sent to your new address so your bird's new avian veterinarian will know your pet's history.

Once you've settled in your new home, develop a rapport with an avian veterinarian in the area and schedule your conure for a new patient exam. That way, you'll know your bird came through the move with flying colors!

PET SITTERS

If you're unsure about what to look for in a pet sitter, Pet-Sitters International offers the following tips:

- Look for a bonded pet sitter who carries commercial liability insurance, references and a written description of services and fees.

- Arrange to have the pet sitter come to your home to meet the pets before you leave on your trip. During the initial interview, evaluate the sitter. Does he or she seem comfortable with your bird? Does the sitter have experience caring for birds? Does he or she own birds?

- Ask for a written contract and discuss the availability of vet care (does he or she have an existing arrangement with your veterinarian, for example).

- Discuss what the sitter's policy is for determining when a pet owner has returned home. Does he or she visit the home until the owners return? Will he or she call to ensure you've arrived home safely and your pets are cared for?

GOING ON VACATION

If your conure enjoys traveling, you may be tempted to take him on vacation with you. This decision I leave entirely in your hands, although I generally do not recommend taking pet birds along on vacations, and I leave my parrot in the care of trusted friends or her avian veterinarian's office when I'm away. I believe most parrots do not find travel enlightening or broadening and are better left in familiar surroundings.

Only leave your bird with a pet sitter who has experience with, or owns, birds.

I have used the services of trusted friends and have boarded my birds at my avian veterinarians'offices. Both have worked out well. In some cases, my friends were experienced bird owners, while others were simply animal lovers who enjoyed the company of my pet as much as I did.

When leaving my parrot with my avian vet, I believe she is in good hands. The staff greets her quite warmly. If something happens to her or if she becomes ill, she's in the right place to be taken care of, and if she has an uneventful few days, she still has six or seven people catering to her every whim instead of only me.

chapter 5

Your Conure's Home

Selecting your conure's cage will be one of the most important decisions you will make for your pet. Where the cage will be located in your home is just as important. Don't wait until you bring your bird home to think this through; you'll want your new pet to settle in to her surroundings right away, rather than adding to her stress by relocating her several times before selecting the right spot.

Here's what you'll need to look for at the pet store to set your conure up right!

- a cage
- food and water bowls (at least two sets of each for easier dish changing and cage cleaning)
- perches of varying diameters and materials

51

- a sturdy scrub brush to clean the perches

- food (a good-quality fresh seed mixture or a formulated diet, such as pellets or crumbles)

- a powdered vitamin and mineral supplement to sprinkle on your pet's fresh foods

- a variety of safe, fun toys

- a cage cover (an old sheet or towel that is free of holes will serve this purpose nicely)

- a play gym to allow your conure time out of her cage and a place to exercise

When you are stocking up for your bird's arrival, don't forget to pick out some safe toys.

Choosing a Cage

When selecting a cage for your conure, make sure the bird has room to spread her wings without touching the cage sides. Her tail should not touch the cage bottom, nor should her head brush the top. A cage that measures 2 feet by 2 feet by 3 feet is the minimum size for a single conure, and bigger is always better.

Examine any cage you choose carefully before making your final selection. If you are choosing a powder-coated cage, make sure that the finish is not chipped, bubbled or peeling, because your pet may find the spot and continue removing the finish, which can cause a cage to look old and worn before its time. Also, your pet could become ill if she ingests any of the finish.

If you are considering a galvanized cage, be aware that some birds can become ill from ingesting pieces of the galvanized wire. You can prevent this "new cage syndrome" by washing down the cage wires thoroughly with a solution of vinegar and water, and then scrubbing the cage with a wire brush to loosen any stray bits of galvanized wire. Rinse the cage thoroughly with water and allow it to dry before putting your bird into her new home.

BAR SPACING

Reject any cages that have sharp interior wires or wide bar spacing. (Recommended bar spacing for conures is about ½ inch.) Sharp wires could poke your bird or she could become caught between bars that are slightly wider than recommended. Also be aware that ornate scrollwork that decorates some cages may be a hazard to your bird. Finally, make sure the cage you choose has several horizontal bars in it because your conure will want to climb the cage walls as part of her exercise routine.

To prevent injury and escape, your conure's cage should have bars spaced about ½ inch apart.

CAGE DOOR

Once you've checked the overall cage quality and the bar spacing, look at the cage door. Does it open easily for you, yet remain secure enough to keep your bird in her cage when you close the door? Some conures become quite good at letting themselves out of their cages if the cage doors do not close securely. If you discover you have a feathered Houdini on your hands, a small padlock may help keep your escape artist in her place.

Other things to consider: Is the door wide enough for you to get your hand in and out of the cage comfortably? Will your bird's food bowl fit through the door easily? In which direction does the door open? Some bird owners prefer that their pets have a play porch on a door that opens drawbridge style, while others are happy with doors that open to the side.

CAGE TRAY

Next, look at the cage tray. Does it slide in and out of the cage easily? Remember that you will be changing the paper in this tray at least once a day for the rest of your bird's life (which could be forty years with good care). Is the tray an odd shape or size? Will paper need to be cut into unusual shapes to fit in it, or will paper towels, newspapers or clean sheets of used computer paper fit easily? The easier the tray is to remove and reline, the more likely you will be to change the lining of the tray daily. Can the cage tray be replaced if it becomes damaged and unusable? Ask the pet-store staff before making your purchase.

For lining the cage tray, I recommend clean black-and-white newsprint, paper towels or clean sheets of used computer printer paper. Sand, ground corncobs or walnut shells may be sold by your pet-supply store, but I don't recommend these as cage flooring materials because they sometimes make owners lazy in their cage-cleaning habits. These materials tend to hide droppings and discarded food quite well, which can cause a bird owner to forget to change the cage tray on the principle that if it doesn't look dirty, it must not be dirty. This line of thinking can set up a thriving, robust colony of bacteria in the bottom of your bird's cage, which can lead to a sick bird if you're not careful. Newsprint and other paper products don't hide the dirt; in fact, they seem to draw attention to it, which leads conscientious bird owners to keep their pets' homes scrupulously clean.

You may see sandpaper or "gravel paper" sold in some pet stores as a cage tray liner. This product is supposed to provide a bird with an opportunity to ingest grit, which is purported to help aid her digestion by providing coarse grinding material that will help break up food in the bird's gizzard. However, many avian experts do not believe that a pet bird needs grit, and if a bird stands on rough sandpaper, she could become prone to foot problems caused by the rough surface of the paper. For your pet's health, please don't use these gravel-coated papers.

You may notice that some of the cages for conures feature cage aprons, which help keep the debris your bird will create in the course of a day off your floor and somewhat under control. Cage aprons make cleaning up after your pet quicker and easier, and they also protect your carpet or flooring from discarded food and bird droppings if your bird decides to perch on the edge of her cage.

Finally, check the floor of the cage you've chosen. Does the cage have a grille that will keep your bird out of the debris that falls to the bottom, such as feces, seed hulls, molted feathers and discarded food? To ensure your pet's long-term good health and to protect your conure from her own curious nature, it's essential to have a grille between your pet and the litter in the cage tray. Also, it's easier to keep your conure in her cage while you're cleaning the cage tray if there's a grille between the cage and the tray.

Where to Put the Cage

Now that you've picked the perfect cage for your pet, where will you put it? Your conure will be happiest when she can feel like she's part of the family, so the living room, family room or dining room may be among the best places for your bird.

Avoid keeping your bird in the bathroom or kitchen, because sudden temperature fluctuations or fumes from cleaning products used in those rooms could harm your pet. Another spot to avoid is a busy hall or entryway, because the activity level in these spots may be too much for your pet.

CAGE CONSIDERATIONS

Your conure will spend much of her time in her cage, so make this environment as stimulating, safe and comfortable as possible. Keep the following things in mind when choosing a good cage for your conure.

- Make sure the cage is big enough. The dimensions of the cage (height, length and depth) should add up to at least 60 inches for a single bird.
- An acrylic cage may mean easier cleanup for the bird owner. Wood or bamboo cages will be quickly destroyed by an eager conure's beak.
- Make sure the cage door opens easily and stays securely open and closed. Avoid "guillotine-style" doors.
- The cage tray should be regularly shaped and easy to slide in and out. There should be a grille covering the cage floor so you can change the substrate without worrying about the bird's escape.

If possible, set up the cage so that it is at your eye level, because it will make servicing the cage and visiting with your pet easier for you. It will also reduce the stress on your conure, because birds like to be up high for security. Also, they do not like to have people or things looming over them, so consider items such as ceiling fans, chandeliers or swag lamps. If members of your family are particularly tall, they may want to sit next to the cage or crouch down slightly to talk to the conure.

Whatever room you select for your conure's cage, be sure to put her in a secure corner (with one solid wall behind the cage to ensure your conure's sense of security) near a window. Please don't put the cage in direct sun, though, because conures can quickly overheat.

Being high up will reduce your conure's stress and give her a feeling of security.

Cage Accessories

Along with the perfect-sized cage in the ideal location   These include food and water dishes, perches, toys and a cage cover.

FOOD AND WATER DISHES

Conures seem to enjoy food crocks, which are open ceramic bowls that allow them to hop up on the edge of the bowl and pick and choose what they will during the day. Crocks are also heavy enough to prevent mischievous birds from upending their food bowls, which can leave the bird hungry and the owner with quite a mess to clean up. You may also want to consider purchasing a cage with locking bowl holders because bowls that are locked in place (but are still easy to remove by bird owners at mealtime) are less likely to be upset by your conure.

If your conure isn't prone to tipping over bowls, she may do well with a clean plastic tray from frozen dinners or a metal pie plate. Be sure to purchase dishes that are less than 1 inch deep to ensure that your bird has easy access to her food at all times. When purchasing dishes for your conure, pick up several sets so that mealtime cleanups are quick and easy.

PERCHES

When choosing perches for your pet's cage, try to buy two different diameters or materials so your bird's feet won't get tired of standing on the same-sized perch of the same material day after day. Think of how tired your feet would feel if you stood on your bare feet on a piece of wood all day, then imagine how it would feel to stand on that piece of wood barefoot every day for years. Sounds pretty uncomfortable, doesn't it? That's basically what your bird has to look forward to if you don't vary her perching choices.

The recommended diameter for conure perches is ¾ inch, so try to buy one perch of that size and one that is slightly larger (1 inch, for example) to give your pet a chance to stretch her foot muscles. Birds spend almost all of their lives standing, so keeping their feet healthy is important. Also, avian foot problems are much easier to prevent than they are to treat.

A crock is great fun for your conure—she'll enjoy perching on the edge while eating.

You'll probably notice a lot of different kinds of perches when you visit your pet store. Along with the traditional wooden dowels, bird owners can now purchase perches made from manzanita branches, PVC tubes, rope and terra-cotta or concrete for grooming.

Manzanita offers birds varied diameters on the same perch, along with chewing possibilities, while PVC is almost indestructible. (Make sure any PVC perches you offer your bird have been scuffed slightly with sandpaper to improve traction on the perch.) Rope perches also offer varied diameter and a softer perching surface than wood or plastic, and terra-cotta and concrete provide slightly abrasive surfaces that birds can use to groom their beaks without severely damaging the skin on their feet in the process. Some bird owners have reported that their pets have suffered foot abrasions with these perches, however; watch your pet carefully for signs of sore feet (an inability to perch or climb, favoring a foot or raw, sore skin on the feet) if you choose to use these perches in your pet's cage. If your bird shows signs of lameness, remove the abrasive perches immediately and have your bird checked by her avian veterinarian.

To promote your conure's comfort and foot health, keep several types of perches in her cage.

To help prevent your bird from developing foot problems, do not use sandpaper covers on her perches. These sleeves, touted as nail trimming devices, really do little to trim a parrot's nails because birds don't usually drag their nails along their perches. What the sandpaper perch covers *are* good at doing, though, is abrading the surface of your conure's feet, which can leave them vulnerable to infections and can make moving about the cage painful for your pet.

When placing perches in your bird's cage, try to vary the heights slightly so your bird has different "levels" in her cage. Don't place any perches over food or water dishes, because birds can and will contaminate food or water by defecating in it. Finally, place one perch higher than the rest for a nighttime sleeping roost. Conures and other parrots like to sleep on the highest point they can find to perch, so please provide this security for your pet.

CAGE COVERS

One important, but sometimes overlooked, accessory is the cage cover. Be sure that you have something to cover your conure's cage with when it's time to put your pet to sleep each night. The act of covering the cage seems to calm many pet birds and convince them that it's really time to go to bed even though they may hear the sounds of an active family in the background. You can also cover your conure's cage during the day to calm her if she becomes frightened or to quiet her if she should burst into loud vocalizations.

You can purchase a cage cover, or you can use an old sheet, blanket or towel that is clean and free of holes. Be aware that some birds like to chew on their cage covers through the cage bars. If your bird does this, replace the cover when it becomes too worn to do its job effectively. Replacing a well-chewed cover will also help keep your bird from becoming entangled in the cover or caught in a ragged clump of threads. Some birds have injured themselves quite severely by becoming caught in a holey cage cover, so help keep your pet safe from this hazard.

Entertaining Your Conure

Your new pet has an active, agile mind that needs regular stimulation and challenges. A bored bird is often a destructive, noisy bird—not an ideal pet. Toys for a conure can be as complex as you care to purchase or as simple as an empty paper towel roll.

INTRODUCING NEW TOYS

Conures are naturally curious, so introducing new toys to them should be a great adventure for the birds. You can set new toys next to your conure's cage to gauge her reaction. If she seems to want to know what the new item is, you can probably put it in the cage almost immediately. If, on the other hand, your conure seems a bit apprehensive about the new toy, leave it by the cage for a few days to allow your pet to adjust to her new plaything.

SAFE TOYS

When selecting toys for your pet, keep a few safety tips in mind. First, is the toy the right size for your bird? Large toys can be intimidating to small birds—the birds may be less likely to play with them. On the other end of the spectrum, larger parrots can easily destroy toys designed for smaller birds, and they can sometimes injure themselves severely in the process.

Next, is the toy safe? Good choices include sturdy wooden toys (either un-dyed or painted with bird-safe vegetable dye or food coloring) strung on closed-link chains or vegetable-tanned leather thongs, and rope toys. If you purchase rope toys for your conure, make sure her nails are trimmed regularly to prevent them from snagging in the rope, and discard the toy when it becomes frayed to prevent accidents from happening.

Climbing toys are great fun for a curious conure.

Unsafe items to watch out for are brittle plastic toys that can be shattered easily by a conure's beak, lead-weighted toys that can be cracked open to expose the dangerous lead to curious birds, loose link chains that can catch toenails or beaks or jingle-type bells that can trap toes, tongues or beaks.

Conures kept as single pets sometimes enjoy mirrored toys. Make sure that any mirrored toy you select is unbreakable because your conure's busy beak will give it quite a workout. If you notice that your conure is becoming fixated on the "pretty bird" in the mirror, you should remove the mirrored toy and replace it with another safe nonmirrored plaything.

Some entertaining toys can be made at home. Give your bird an empty paper towel roll or toilet paper tube (from unscented paper only, please), string some Cheerios on a piece of vegetable-tanned leather or offer your bird a dish of raw pasta pieces to destroy.

GAMES

Along with toys, you can play games with your conure to amuse her and yourself.

A variation on the old **"shell game"** from the carnival sideshow is a fun game for your bird. In the avian version, you can hide a favorite treat under a nut cup or paper muffin cup and let your bird guess which shell hides the prize.

The great escape: Offer your bird a clean, knotted-up piece of rope or vegetable-tanned leather and see how long it takes your pet to untie the knots. Give your bird extra points if she doesn't chew through any of the knots to untie them.

The mechanic: Give your conure a clean nut and bolt with the nut screwed on and see how long it takes your bird to undo the nut. Make sure the nut and bolt are large enough that your pet won't swallow either accidentally while playing.

Peek-a-boo: Put a beach towel loosely over your conure, then let the bird work her way out from under it. Heap lavish amounts of praise on your pet for being so clever as to find her way out.

Tug-of-war: Give your bird one end of an empty paper towel roll and tug gently. Chances are your parrot won't easily let go, or if she does, she will quickly be back for more!

In addition to playing games with you, you should encourage your conure to learn how to entertain herself from an early age so she

Keep your conure's nails trim to prevent painful snagging on toys.

does not become overly dependent on you, because this overdependence may lead to screaming, feather picking or other behavioral problems if the bird feels neglected.

As additional entertainment, offer your conure an interesting variety of food, both in the morning and in the evening. Make your pet "work" for some of her food to make mealtime mentally stimulating. Offer peas in the pod, peanuts or other nuts in the shell or whole green beans.

61

THE PLAY GYM

Although your conure will spend quite a bit of time in her cage, she will also need time out of her cage to exercise and to enjoy a change of scenery. A play gym can help keep your pet physically and mentally active.

If you visit a large pet store or bird specialty store, or if you look through the pages of any pet-bird hobbyist magazine, you will see a variety of play gyms on display. You can choose a complicated gym with a series of ladders, swings, perches and toys, or you can purchase a simple T-stand that has a place for food and water bowls and an eyescrew or two from which you can hang toys. If you're really handy with tools, you can even construct a gym to your conure's specifications. The choice is up to you.

As with the cage, location of your conure's play gym is an important consideration. You should try to place the gym in a secure location in your home that is safe from other curious pets, ceiling fans, open windows and other household hazards.

A play gym is a fun spot for your conures to preen, play or even take a nap.

You should also place the gym in a spot frequented by your family, so your bird will have company while she plays and supervision so she doesn't get herself into trouble.

Feeding
Your
Conure

Conures can live to be 40 years of age, but many pet birds do not live past age 15. In the past, when most pet conures were caught in the wild and imported, they rarely survived past the age of 10 due to their diet. Besides shortening a bird's life

span, a poor diet causes a number of health problems, including respiratory infections, poor feather condition, flaky skin and reproductive problems.

The good news for conure owners is that these birds are not known to be particularly fussy when it comes to food. They eat a wide variety of things and are not as shy about trying new foods as other parrot species may be.

Vitamins

According to avian veterinarian Gary Gallerstein, birds require about a dozen vitamins—A, D, E, K, B_1, B_2, niacin, B_6, B_{12}, pantothenic acid, biotin, folic acid and choline—to stay healthy. Of these, they can only partially manufacture vitamin D_3 and niacin. A balanced diet can help provide the rest.

Along with the vitamins listed above, pet birds need trace amounts of some minerals to maintain good health. These minerals are calcium, phosphorus, sodium, chlorine, potassium, magnesium, iron, zinc, copper, sulfur, iodine and manganese. These can be provided with a well-balanced diet and a supplemental mineral block or cuttlebone.

Your conure's diet should include seed, grain, legumes, vegetables and fruit.

A Balanced Diet

Ideally, your conure's diet should contain about equal parts of seed, grain, legumes and dark green or dark orange vegetables and fruits. You can supplement these with small amounts of well-cooked meat or eggs, or dairy products. Let's look at each part of this diet in a little more detail.

First, the seeds, grain and legumes portion of your bird's diet can include clean, fresh seed from your local pet-supply store. Try to buy your birdseed from a store where stock turns over quickly. The dusty box on the bottom shelf of a store with little traffic isn't as nutritious for your pet as a bulk purchase of seeds from a freshly filled bin in a busy shop. When you bring the seeds home, refrigerate them to keep them from becoming infested with seed moths.

To ensure that your bird is receiving the proper nutrients from his diet, you need to know if the seed you're serving is fresh. One way to do this is to try sprouting some of the seeds. Many conures particularly enjoy sprouted seeds, so consider offering your bird regular helpings of this healthful treat!

Be sure that you remove seed hulls from your conure's bowl and refill with fresh seeds daily.

SEEDS

Be sure, too, that your pet has an adequate supply of seeds in his dish at all times. Rather than just looking in the dish while it's in the cage, I suggest that you take the dish out and inspect it over the trash can so you can empty the seed hulls and refill the dish easily. Other items in this group that you can offer your pet include unsweetened breakfast cereals, whole-wheat bread, cooked beans, cooked rice and pasta.

MILLET AND MUNG BEANS

One foodstuff that is very popular with conures is millet, especially millet sprays. These golden sprays are part treat and part toy. Offer your pet this treat sparingly, however, because it is high in fat. Another food that is quite

SPROUTING SEEDS

To sprout seeds, you will need to soak them overnight in some lukewarm water. Drain the water off and let the seeds sit in a closed cupboard or other out-of-the-way place for twenty-four hours. Fresh seeds will sprout; stale seeds won't. Rinse the sprouted seeds thoroughly before offering them to your bird. If the seeds don't sprout, they aren't fresh, and you'll need to find another source for your bird's food. Immediately discard any sprouts that smell funny or grow mold; these are unhealthy to feed to your conure.

popular with many conures is mung beans. Ask for
them at your pet store and, if you're unsuccessful,
check with a health food store in your area.

FRUITS AND VEGETABLES

Dark green or dark orange vegetables and fruits contain vitamin A, an important part of a bird's diet that is
missing from the seeds, grains and legumes group.
This vitamin helps fight off infection and keeps a bird's
eyes, mouth and respira-
tory system healthy. Some
vitamin-A-rich foods are
carrots, yams, sweet potatoes, broccoli, dried red
peppers and dandelion
greens.

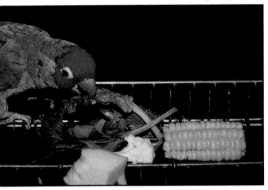

*Fruits and vege-
tables provide
important vita-
mins that your
conure needs for
good health.*

You may be wondering
whether or not to offer
frozen or canned vegeta-
bles and fruits to your
bird. The high sodium content in some canned foods
may make them unhealthy for your conure. Frozen
and canned foods will serve your bird's needs in an
emergency, but I would offer only fresh foods on a regular basis.

PROTEIN

Along with small portions of well-cooked meat you can
also offer your bird bits of tofu, water-packed tuna,
fully scrambled eggs, cottage cheese, unsweetened yo-
gurt or low-fat cheese. Don't overdo the dairy products, though, because a bird's digestive system lacks the
enzyme lactase, which means he is unable to fully
process dairy foods.

Introduce young conures to healthy people food early
so that they learn to appreciate a varied diet. Some
adult birds cling tenaciously to seed-only diets, which
aren't as healthy for them long term. Offer adult birds
fresh foods, too, in the hope that they may try something new.

If your conure's diet is mostly seeds and fresh foods, you may want to sprinkle a good-quality vitamin-and-mineral powder onto the fresh foods, where it has the best chance of sticking to the food and being eaten. Vitamin-enriched seed diets may provide some supplementation, but some of them add the vitamins and minerals to the seed hull, which your pet will discard while he's eating. Avoid adding vitamin and mineral supplements to your bird's water dish, because they can act as a growth medium for bacteria. They may also cause the water to taste different to your bird, which may discourage him from drinking.

> ### FRESHNESS COUNTS
>
> Whatever healthy, fresh foods you offer your pet, be sure to remove food from the cage promptly to prevent spoilage and to help keep your bird healthy. Ideally, you should change the food in your bird's cage every two to four hours (about every thirty minutes in warm weather), so a conure should be all right with a tray of food to pick through in the morning, another to select from during the afternoon and a third fresh salad to nibble on for dinner.

WATER

Along with providing a variety of fresh food at least twice a day, you will need to provide your conure with fresh, clean water twice a day to maintain his good health. You may want to provide your bird water in a shallow dish, or you may find that a water bottle does the trick. If you are considering a water bottle, be aware that some clever conures have been known to stuff a seed into the drinking tube, which allows all the water to drain out of the bottle. This creates a thirsty bird and a soggy cage, neither of which are ideal situations.

Off Limits

Now that we've looked at foods that are good for your bird, let's look briefly at those that aren't healthy for your pet. Among those *foods considered harmful to pet birds* are alcohol, rhubarb and avocado (the skin and the area around the pit can be toxic), as well as highly salted, sweetened or fatty foods. You should especially avoid chocolate because it contains a chemical, theobromine, which birds cannot digest as completely as people can. Chocolate can kill your conure, so resist the temptation to share this snack with your pet. You will also want to avoid giving your bird seeds or pits from apples, apricots, cherries, peaches, pears and plums, because they can be harmful to your pet's health.

Your conure needs fresh food and water at least twice a day.

Let common sense be your guide in choosing which foods can be offered to your bird: If it's healthy for you, it's probably okay to share. However, remember to reduce the size of the portion you offer to your bird—a smaller, conure-sized portion will be more appealing to your pet than a larger, human-sized portion.

While sharing healthy people food with your bird is completely acceptable, sharing something that you've already taken a bite of is not. Human saliva has bacteria in it that are perfectly normal for people but that are potentially toxic to birds, so please don't share partially eaten food with your pet. For your bird's health and your peace of mind, get him his own portion or plate.

The Pelleted Diet Option

Pelleted diets are created by mixing as many as forty different nutrients into a mash and then forcing the hot mixture through a machine to form various shapes. Some pelleted diets have colors and flavors added, while others are fairly plain.

These formulated diets provide more balanced nutrition for your pet bird in an easy-to-serve form that reduces the amount of wasted food and eliminates the chance for a bird to pick through a smorgasbord of healthy foods to find his favorites and reject the foods he isn't particularly fond of. Some conures accept pelleted diets quickly, while others require some persuading.

To convert your pet to a pelleted diet, offer pellets alongside of or mixed in with his current diet. Once you see that your bird is eating the pellets, begin to gradually increase the amount of pellets you offer at mealtime while decreasing the amount of other food you serve. Within a couple of weeks, your bird should be eating his pellets with gusto!

Although most conures aren't shy about trying new foods, yours may be hesitant to accept pellets. If your conure seems a bit finicky about trying pellets, another bird in the house may show your conure how yummy pellets can be, or you may have to act as if you are enjoying the pellets as a snack in front of your pet. Really play up your apparent enjoyment of this new food because it will pique your bird's curiosity and make the pellets exceedingly interesting to your pet.

Introduce pellets into your conure's diet slowly—it may take some time for him to accept a new food.

Whatever you do, don't starve your bird into trying a new food. Offer new foods along with familiar favorites. This will ensure that your bird is eating and will also encourage him to try new foods. Don't be discouraged if your conure doesn't dive right in to a new food. Be patient, keep offering new foods to your bird, and praise him enthusiastically when he samples something new!

7

Grooming
Your
Conure

Your conure has several grooming needs. First, she should be able to bathe regularly, and she will need to have her nails and flight feathers trimmed periodically to ensure her safety.

Although you might think that your conure's beak also needs trimming, I would argue that a healthy bird supplied with enough chew toys seems to do a remarkable job of keeping her beak trimmed. However, if your bird's beak becomes overgrown, please consult your avian veterinarian. A parrot's beak contains a surprising number of blood vessels, so beak trimming is best left to the experts. Also, a suddenly overgrown beak may indicate that your bird is suffering from liver damage, a virus or scaly mites, all of which require veterinary care.

Conures Love Water

As a general rule, conures are true water babies that can't get enough of being wet! If they can't bathe in their water bowl or under the faucet in the kitchen or bath, they may take a quick roll through their food bowl, especially if there are a lot of damp, dark-green, leafy vegetables in it. You may notice that your bird is particularly motivated to bathe when you vacuum the room in which she lives. Experts think that the sound of a vacuum in the home reminds conures of some distant time when they lived in the jungles and thunderstorms were brewing.

Regardless of the means you use, be sure to set bath time early enough in the day so your pet's feathers can dry before bedtime, or you can use a blow dryer set on low to help the process along.

Unless your conure has gotten herself into oil,

Conures are always ready to bathe—they are true water babies!

paint, wax or some other substance that elbow grease alone won't remove and that could harm her feathers, she will not require soap as part of her bath. Under routine conditions, soaps and detergents can damage a bird's feathers by removing beneficial oils, so hold the shampoo during your conure's normal clean-up routine!

About Mite Protectors

While we're discussing grooming and feather care, please don't purchase mite protectors that hang on a bird's cage or conditioning products that are applied directly to a bird's feathers. Well-cared-for conures don't have mites and shouldn't be in danger of contracting them. (If your pet does have mites, veterinary care is the most effective treatment method.) Also, the fumes from some of these products are quite strong and can be harmful to your pet's health.

Nail Clipping

Conures need their nails clipped occasionally to prevent the nails from catching on toys or perches and injuring the bird. You will need to remove only tiny portions of the nail to keep your conure's claws trimmed. Generally, a good guideline to follow is to only remove the hook on each nail, and to do this in the smallest increments possible.

You may find that you have better luck filing your bird's nails with an emery board than with conventional nail clippers. Whatever method you choose to use, stop trimming well before you reach the quick, which is difficult to see in a conure's black toenails. If you do happen to cut the nail short enough to make it bleed, apply cornstarch or flour, followed by direct pressure, to stop the bleeding.

When clipping your conure's nails, remove the hook on each nail in small amounts.

Wing Trimming

The goal of a properly done wing trim is to prevent your bird from flying away or flying into a window, mirror or wall while she's out of her cage. An added benefit of trimming your pet's wings is that her inability to fly well will make her more dependent on you for transportation, which should make her more handleable. However, the bird still needs enough wing feathers so that she can glide safely to the ground if she is startled and takes flight from her cage top or play gym.

Because proper wing trimming is a delicate balance, you may want to enlist the help of your avian veterinarian, at least the first time. Wing trimming is a task that must be performed carefully to avoid injuring your pet, so take your time if you're doing it yourself. Please **do not** just

ENCOURAGE PREENING

If you want to encourage your bird to preen regularly and help condition her feathers, simply mist her regularly with clean, warm water or hold her under a gentle stream from a kitchen or bathroom faucet. Your bird will take care of the rest.

take up the largest pair of kitchen shears you own and start snipping away. I have heard stories from avian veterinarians about birds whose owners cut off their birds' wing tips (down to the bone) in this manner.

The first step in wing feather trimming is to assemble all the things you will need and find a quiet, well-lit place to groom your pet before you catch and trim her. Your grooming tools will include:

- a well-worn towel to wrap your bird in

- small, sharp scissors to do the actual trimming

- needle-nosed pliers (to pull any blood feathers you may cut accidentally)

- flour or cornstarch to act as styptic powder in case a blood feather is cut

Keeping your conure's wings trimmed will make her more dependent on you and easier to handle.

I encourage you to groom your pet in a quiet, well-lit place because grooming excites some birds and causes them to become unsettled. Having good light to work under will make your job easier, and having a quiet work area may just calm down your pet and make her a bit easier to handle.

Once you've assembled your supplies, drape the towel over your hand and catch your bird with your toweled hand. Grab your bird by the back of her head and neck, and wrap her in the towel. Hold your bird's head securely with your thumb and index finger. (Having the bird's head covered by the towel will calm her and

73

will give her something to chew on while you clip her wings.)

Lay the bird on her back, being careful not to constrict or compress her chest (remember, birds have no diaphragms to help them breathe) and spread her wing out carefully to look for blood feathers that are still growing in. These can be identified by their waxy, tight look and their dark centers or quills, which are caused by the blood supply to the new feather.

GROOMING TIPS

- Groom your pet in a quiet, well-lit place.

- Have all the necessary grooming supplies close by before you begin.

- Make sure you have styptic powder on hand.

- Check wings and toenails regularly to see if they need trimming.

If your bird has a number of blood feathers, you may want to put off trimming her wings for a few days, because fully grown feathers cushion those just coming in. If your bird has only one or two blood feathers, you can trim the rest accordingly.

To trim your bird's feathers, separate each one from the other flight feathers and cut it individually (remember, the goal is to have a well-trimmed bird that's still able to glide a bit if she needs to). Use the primary coverts (the set of feathers above the primary flight feathers on your bird's wing) as a guideline for how short you can trim.

Cut the first six to eight flight feathers starting from the tip of the wing, and be sure to trim an equal number of feathers from each wing. Although some people think that a bird needs only one trimmed wing, this is incorrect and could actually cause harm to a bird that tries to fly with one trimmed and one untrimmed wing.

BLOOD FEATHERS

If you do happen to cut a blood feather, remain calm. You must remove it and stop the bleeding, and panicking will do neither you nor your bird much good.

To remove a blood feather, take a pair of needle-nosed pliers and grasp the broken feather's shaft as close to the skin of your bird's wing as you can. With one steady motion, pull the feather out completely. After you've removed the feather, put a pinch of flour or cornstarch on the feather follicle (the spot from which you pulled the feather) and apply direct pressure for a few minutes until the bleeding stops. If the bleeding doesn't stop after a few minutes of direct pressure, or if you can't remove the feather shaft, contact your avian veterinarian for further instructions.

You'll know it's time to trim your conure's flight feathers when she starts making brave attempts to fly.

Although it may seem like you're hurting your conure by removing the broken blood feather, consider this: A broken blood feather is like an open faucet. If the feather stays in, the faucet remains open and lets the blood out. Once removed, the bird's skin generally closes up behind the feather shaft and shuts off the faucet.

You must remember to check your bird's wing feathers and retrim them periodically (about four times a year as a minimum). Be particularly alert after a molt, because your bird will have a whole new crop of flight feathers that needs attention. You'll be able to tell when your bird is due for a trim when she starts becoming bolder in her flying attempts. Right after a wing trim, a conure generally tries to fly and finds she's unsuccessful at the attempt. She will keep trying, though, and may surprise you one day with a fairly good glide across her cage or off her play gym. If this happens, get the scissors and trim those wings immediately.

RECOVERING A LOST BIRD

If, despite your best efforts, your bird should escape, you must act quickly for the best chance of recovering your pet. Here are some things to keep in mind:

- If possible, keep the bird in sight. This will make chasing her easier.

- Have an audio tape of your bird's voice and a portable tape recorder available to lure your bird back home.

- Place your bird's cage in an area where your bird is likely to see it, such as on a deck or patio. Put lots of treats and food on the floor of the cage to tempt your pet back into her home.

- Use another caged bird to attract your conure's attention.

- Alert your avian veterinarian's office, the local humane society and other veterinary offices in your area that your bird has escaped.

- Post fliers in your neighborhood describing your bird. Offer a reward and include your phone number.

- Don't give up hope.

If Your Bird Flies Away . . .

One of the most common accidents that befalls bird owners is when a fully flighted bird escapes through an open door or window. Just because your bird has never flown before or shown any interest in leaving her cage doesn't mean that she can't fly or that she won't become disoriented once she's outside. If you don't believe it can happen, just check the lost and found advertisements in your local newspaper for a week. Chances are many birds will turn up in the lost column, but few are ever found.

WHERE DID SHE GO?

Why do lost birds never return home? Some birds fall victim to predatory animals in the wild, while others join flocks of feral, or wild, parrots (Florida and California are particularly noted for these). Still other lost birds end up flying wildly and frantically in any direction. They are eventually found by people who are too far away from the bird's home to access the owner's lost-bird advertisements. Finally, some people who find lost birds don't advertise that they've been found because the finders think that whoever was unlucky or uncaring enough to lose the bird in the first place doesn't deserve to have her back.

How can you prevent your bird from becoming lost? First, make sure her wings are safely trimmed at regular intervals. Be sure to trim both wings evenly and remember to trim wings after your bird has molted.

Next, be sure your bird's cage door locks securely and that her cage tray cannot come loose if the cage is knocked over or dropped accidentally. Also be sure that all your window screens fit securely and are free from tears and large holes. Keep all window screens and patio doors closed when your bird is out of her cage. Finally, never go outside with your bird on your shoulder.

Remember to take precautions against losing your bird in case she decides to take flight.

chapter 8

Keeping
Your **Conure**
Healthy

You may be surprised to find out that your body has a lot in common with your conure's body. You both have skin; a skeleton; respiratory, cardiovascular, digestive, excretory and nervous systems and sensory organs, although the various systems function in slightly different ways.

Avian Anatomy

Your conure's skin is probably pretty difficult to see since your pet has so many feathers. If you part the feathers carefully, though, you can see your bird's thin, seemingly transparent skin and the muscles beneath it. Modified skin cells help make up your bird's beak, cere, claws and the scales on his feet and legs.

YOUR BIRD'S SKELETON

Next, let's look at your bird's skeleton. Did you know that some bird bones are hollow? They are, which means that they are lighter (making flying easier), but it also means that these bones may be more susceptible to breakage. For this reason, you must always handle your bird carefully! Another adaptation for flight is that the bones of a bird's wing (which correspond to our arm and hand bones) are fused for greater strength.

Having three additional vertebrae gives birds the ability to turn their heads almost 180°.

Birds also have air sacs in some of their bones (these are called pneumatic bones) and throughout their bodies that help lighten the bird's body and cool it more efficiently. Birds cannot perspire in the same way that mammals do because birds have no sweat glands, so they must have an alternate way to cool themselves off.

Parrots have ten neck vertebrae in contrast with a human's seven. This gives a parrot's neck a greater range of movement than a person's (a parrot can turn his head almost 180°), which can be an advantage in spotting food or predators in the wild.

COOLING OFF

On a warm day, you may notice your bird sitting with his wings held away from his body, rolling his tongue and holding his mouth open. This is how a bird cools himself off. Watch your bird carefully on warm days because he can overheat quickly, and he may suffer heatstroke, which can require veterinary care. If you live in a warm climate, ask your avian veterinarian how you can protect your bird from this potentially serious problem.

During breeding season, a female bird's bones become denser as they store calcium needed to create eggshells. A female's skeleton can weigh up to 20 percent more during breeding season than it does the rest of the year because of this calcium storage. If you set up conures for breeding, do not allow hens to rear more than two clutches of chicks per year to keep them from depleting their calcium reserves.

RESPIRATORY SYSTEM

Your bird's respiratory system is a highly efficient system that works in a markedly different way from yours. Here's how your bird breathes: Air enters the system through your bird's nares, passes through his sinuses and into his throat. As it does, the air is filtered through the **choana**, which is a slit that can be easily seen in the roof of many birds' mouths. The choana also helps to clean and warm the air before it goes further into the respiratory system.

Two complete breaths are necessary for your conure to inhale and exhale.

After the air passes the choana, it flows through the larynx and trachea, past the **syrinx** or "voice box." Your bird doesn't have vocal cords like you do; rather, vibrations of the syrinx membrane are what allow birds to make sounds.

So far it sounds similar to the way we breathe, doesn't it? Well, here's where the differences begin. As the air continues its journey past the syrinx and into the bronchi, your bird's **lungs** don't expand and contract to bring the air in. This is partly due to the fact that birds don't have diaphragms like people do. Instead, the bird's body wall expands and contracts, much like a fireplace bellows. This action brings air into the air sacs mentioned earlier as part of the skeleton. This bellows action also moves air in and out of the lungs.

Although a bird's respiratory system is extremely efficient at exchanging gases in the system, two complete breaths are required to do the same work that a single breath does in people and other mammals. This is why you may notice that your bird seems to be breathing quite quickly.

CARDIOVASCULAR SYSTEM

Along with the respiratory system, your bird's cardiovascular system keeps oxygen and other nutrients moving throughout your pet's body, although the circulatory path in your conure differs from yours. In your pet bird, the blood that flows from the legs, reproductive system and lower intestines passes

You may notice that your bird's feet are hot— that's because his body temperature is higher than yours.

through the kidneys on its way back to the general circulatory system.

Like you, though, your conure has a four-chambered heart, with two atria and two ventricles. Unlike your average heart rate of 72 beats per minute, your conure's average heart rate is 340 to 600 beats per minute.

DIGESTIVE SYSTEM

To keep this energy-efficient machine (your bird's body) running, the digestive system provides fuel via food. One of the main functions of the digestive system is to provide the fuel that maintains your bird's body temperature. A bird's body temperature is higher than a human's. You may notice that your bird has "hot" feet due to this normal body temperature.

Your conure's digestive system begins with his **beak**. The size and shape of a bird's beak depend on his food-gathering needs. Compare and contrast the sharp, pointed beak of an eagle or the elongated bill of a hummingbird with the hooked beak of your parrot.

Notice the underside of your bird's upper beak if you can. It has tiny ridges in it that help your conure hold and crack seeds more easily.

Parrots don't have saliva to help break down and move their food around like we do. Also, their taste buds are contained in the roofs of their mouths. Because they have few taste buds, experts think that a parrot's sense of taste is poorly developed.

After the food leaves your bird's mouth, it travels down the **esophagus**, where it is moistened. The food then travels to the **crop**, where it is moistened further and is supplied in small increments to the bird's stomach.

After the food leaves the crop, it travels through the **proventriculus**, where digestive juices are added, to the **gizzard**, where the food is broken down into even smaller pieces. The food then travels to the **small intestine**, where nutrients are absorbed into the bloodstream. Anything that's leftover then travels through the large intestine to the **cloaca**, which is the common chamber that collects wastes before they leave the bird's body through the vent.

Along with the solid waste created by the digestive system, your conure's kidneys create urine, which is then transported through ureters to the cloaca for excretion. Unlike a mammal, a bird does not have a bladder or a urethra.

Nervous System

Your conure's nervous system is very similar to your own. Both are made up of the brain, the spinal cord and countless nerves throughout the body that transmit messages to and from the brain.

Feathers

Now that we've examined some of the similarities between avian and human anatomy, let's stop and look at some of the unusual anatomical features birds have. The first feature I'd like to discuss is probably one of the reasons you're attracted to birds: feathers. Birds are the only animals that have feathers, which serve several purposes. Feathers help birds fly, they keep birds warm, they attract the attention of potential mates and they help scare away predators.

Did you know that your conure has between 2,000 and 3,000 feathers on his body? These feathers grow from follicles that are arranged in rows known as pterylae. The unfeathered patches of bare skin on your conure's body are called apteria.

A feather is a remarkably designed creation. The base of the feather shaft, which fits into the bird's skin, is called the **quill**. It is light and hollow, but remarkably tough. The upper part of the feather shaft is called the **rachis**. From it branch the **barbs** and barbules (smaller barbs) that make up most of the feather. The barbs and barbules have small hooks on them that enable the different parts of the feather to interlock like Velcro and form the feather's vane or web.

Besides keeping your conure warm, feathers help to protect him from predators and to attract potential mates.

Birds have several different types of feathers on their bodies. **Contour feathers** are the colorful outer feathers on a bird's body and wings. Many birds have an undercoating of **down feathers** that help keep them warm. **Semiplume feathers** are found on a bird's beak, nares (nostrils) and eyelids.

A bird's **flight feathers** can be classified as one of two types. Primary flight feathers are the large wing feathers that push a bird forward during flight. They are

83

also the ones that need clipping, which is discussed in chapter 7. Secondary flight feathers are found on the inner wing, and they help support the bird in flight. Primary and secondary wing feathers can operate independently of each other. The bird's **tail feathers** also assist in flight by acting as a brake and a rudder to make steering easier.

To keep their feathers in good condition, healthy birds will spend a great deal of time fluffing their feathers and preening them. You may see your conure seeming to pick at the base of his tail on the top side. This is a normal behavior in which the bird removes oil from the preen gland and spreads it on his feathers. The oil also helps prevent skin infections and waterproofs the feathers.

Preening is a normal behavior that helps keep your bird's feathers in top shape.

Sometimes pet birds will develop white lines or small holes on the large feathers of their wings and tails. These lines or holes are referred to as "stress bars" or "stress lines" and result from the bird being under stress as the feathers were developing. If you notice stress bars on your conure's feathers, discuss them with your avian veterinarian. Be prepared to tell the doctor about anything new in your conure's routine, because parrots are creatures of habit that sometimes react badly to changes in their surroundings, diet or daily activities. I find stress bars on my parrot's feathers each time she completes a course of antibiotic treatments, and I also find stress bars on her tail feathers regularly. I attribute the stress bars in her tail to the fact that she is a rather clumsy parrot and often catches or bends her developing tail feathers in the cage bars and floor grate.

Conure Senses

Sight

Although a bird has a poor sense of taste, he has a well-developed sense of sight. Birds can see detail and they can discern colors. Be aware of this when selecting cage accessories for your pet, because some birds react to a change in the color of their food dishes. Some seem excited by a different color bowl, while others act fearful of the new item. Sindbad, for example, recognizes her black food trays and her red, blue, brown or ivory water bowls, but if I offer her food or water in a different color tray or bowl, she is hesitant to eat or drink right away. She must become accustomed to the new food vessel before she eats or drinks, a process that can take as little as a few minutes or as long as half a day.

Because their eyes are located on the sides of their heads, most pet birds rely on monocular vision, which means that they use each eye independently of the other. If a bird really wants to study an object, you will often see him tilt his head to one side and examine the object with just one eye.

Like cats and dogs, birds have third eyelids called nictitating membranes, which you will sometimes see flick briefly across your parrot's eye. The purpose of this membrane is to keep the eyeball moist and clean. If you see your bird's nictitating membrane for more than a brief second, please contact your avian veterinarian for an evaluation. You have probably noticed that your bird lacks eyelashes. In their place are small feathers called semiplumes that help keep dirt and dust out of the bird's eyeball.

HEARING

You may be wondering where your conure's ears are. Look carefully under the feathers behind and below each eye to find them. The ears are the somewhat large holes in the sides of your parrot's head. Conures have about the same ability to distinguish sound waves and determine the location of the sound as people do, but birds seem to be less sensitive to higher and lower pitches than their owners.

TASTE AND SMELL

Birds seem to have poorly developed senses of smell and taste because smells often dissipate quickly in the air (where flying birds spend their time) and because birds have fewer taste buds in their mouths than people do. (Parrot taste buds are located in the roof of the birds' mouths, not in the tongue like ours are.)

TOUCH

Your bird may use his feet or his mouth to investigate an interesting item.

The final sense we relate to, touch, is well-developed in parrots. Parrots use their feet and their mouths to touch their surroundings (young birds particularly seem to "mouth" everything they can get their beaks on), to play and to determine what is safe to perch on or chew on and what's good to eat.

Along with their tactile uses, a parrot's feet also have an unusual design compared to other caged birds. Two of your bird's toes point forward and two point backward. This arrangement is called zygodactyl, and it allows a parrot to hold food or toys in his foot and to climb around easily.

Visiting the Veterinarian

With good care, a conure can live up to 40 years, although the average life span of a pet conure is about 15 years. One of the reasons conures don't live longer is that their owners may be reluctant to take their pets to the veterinarian. Some people don't want to pay veterinary bills on comparatively "inexpensive" birds.

CHOOSING A VETERINARIAN

As a caring owner, you want your bird to have good care and the best chance of living a long, healthy life. To that end, you will need to locate a veterinarian who understands the special medical needs of birds and with whom you can establish a good working relationship.

The best time to do this is when you first bring your bird home from the breeder or pet store. If possible, arrange to visit your veterinarian's office on your way home from the breeder or store. This is particularly important if you have other birds at home, because you don't want to endanger the health of your existing flock or your new pet.

If you don't know an avian veterinarian in your area, ask the person you bought your conure from where he or she takes his or her birds.(Breeders and bird stores

usually have avian veterinarians on whom they depend.) Talk to other bird owners you know and find out whom they take their pets to, or call bird clubs in your area for referrals.

If you don't have friends who own birds, or can't locate a bird club, your next best bet is the yellow pages. Read the advertisements for veterinarians carefully, and try to find one who specializes in birds. Many veterinarians who have an interest in treating birds will join the Association of Avian Veterinarians and advertise themselves as members of this organization. Some veterinarians have taken and passed a special examination that entitles them to be called avian specialists.

It is important that you find a veterinarian who has been trained specifically to care for the medical needs of birds.

Once you've received your recommendations or have found likely candidates in the telephone book, start calling the veterinary offices. Ask the receptionist how many birds the doctor sees in a week or month, how much an office visit costs and what payment options are available (cash, credit card, check or time payments). You can also inquire if the doctor keeps birds as his or her personal pets.

If you like the answers you receive from the receptionist, make an appointment for your parrot to be evaluated. Make a list of any questions you want to ask the doctor regarding diet, how often your bird's wings and nails should be clipped or how often you should bring the bird in for an examination. Take the list with you at the time of your first office visit so you will remember to ask the doctor all of your questions.

Plan to arrive a little early for your first appointment because you will be asked to fill out a patient information form. This form will ask you for your bird's name, his age and sex, the length of time you have owned him, your name, address and telephone number, your preferred method of paying for veterinary services, how you heard about the veterinary office and the name and address of a friend the veterinary office can contact in case of emergency. The form may also ask you to express your opinion on the amount of money you would spend on your pet in an emergency, because this can help the doctor know what kind of treatment to recommend should an emergency arise.

Bird owners should not be afraid to ask their avian veterinarians questions. Avian vets have devoted a lot of time, energy and effort to studying birds, so put this resource to use whenever you can.

PREPARING FOR A VISIT TO THE VETERINARIAN

What bird owners may not know is that they may be asked a number of questions by the veterinarian. When you take your bird in for an exam, be aware that the doctor may ask you for answers to these questions:

- Why is the bird here today?

- What's the bird's normal activity level like?

- How is the bird's appetite?

- What does the bird's normal diet consist of?

- Have you noticed a change in the bird's appearance lately?

Be sure to explain any changes in as much detail as you can, because changes in your bird's normal behavior can indicate illness.

Your Bird's First Examination

During the initial examination, the veterinarian will probably take his or her first look at your parrot while he is still in his cage or carrier. The doctor may talk to you and your bird for a few minutes to give the bird an opportunity to become accustomed to him or her, rather than simply reaching right in and grabbing your pet. While the veterinarian is talking to you, he or she will check the bird's posture and his ability to perch.

Next, the doctor should remove the bird from his carrier or cage and look him over carefully. He or she will particularly note the condition of your pet's eyes, his beak and his nares (nostrils). The bird should be weighed, and the veterinarian will probably palpate (feel) your parrot's body and wings for any lumps, bumps or deformities that require further investigation. Feather condition will also be assessed, as will the condition of the bird's vent, legs and feet.

Common Medical Tests for Birds

After your veterinarian has completed your conure's physical examination, he or she may recommend further tests. These can include:

- Blood work-ups, which help a doctor determine if your bird has a specific disease. Blood tests can be further broken down into a complete blood count, which determines how many platelets, red and white blood cells, your bird has (this information can help diagnose infections or anemia), and a blood chemistry profile, which helps a veterinarian analyze how your bird's body processes enzymes, electrolytes and other chemicals.

- Radiographs or x-rays, which allow a veterinarian to study the size and shape of a bird's internal organs, along with the formation of his bones. X-rays also help doctors find foreign bodies in a bird's system.

- Microbiological exams, which help a veterinarian determine if any unusual organisms (bacteria, fungi or yeast) are growing inside your bird's body.

• Fecal analysis, which studies a small sample of your bird's droppings to determine if he has internal parasites, or a bacterial or yeast infection.

FOLLOW-UP HEALTH CARE

Monitor your conure's daily routine—if something changes, contact his avian veterinarian.

Once the examination is concluded and you've had a chance to discuss any questions you have with your veterinarian, the doctor will probably recommend a follow-up examination schedule for your pet. Most healthy birds visit the veterinarian annually, but some have to go more frequently.

To help your veterinarian and to keep your pet from suffering long-term health risks, keep a close eye on his daily activities and appearance. If something suddenly changes in the way your bird looks or acts, contact your veterinarian immediately. Birds naturally hide signs of illness to protect them from predators, so by the time a bird looks or acts sick, he may already be dangerously ill.

Medicating Your Conure

Most bird owners are faced with the prospect of medicating their pets at some point in the birds' lives, and many are unsure if they can complete the task without hurting their pets. If you have to medicate your pet, your avian veterinarian or veterinary technician should explain the process to you. In the course of the explanation, you should find out how you will be administering the medication, how much of a given drug you will be giving your bird, how often the bird needs the medication and how long the entire course of treatment will last.

If you find (as I often have) that you've forgotten one or more of these steps after you arrive home with your bird and your instructions, call your vet's office for clarification to ensure that your bird receives the follow-up care from you that he needs to recover.

Let's briefly review the most common methods of administering medications to birds, which are discussed completely in *The Complete Bird Owner's Handbook* by Gary A. Gallerstein, D.V.M. They are:

ORAL MEDICATION

This is a good method of medicating birds that are small, easy to handle or underweight. The medication is usually given with a needleless plastic syringe placed in the left side of the bird's mouth and pointed toward the right side of his throat. This route is recommended to ensure that the medication gets into the bird's digestive system and not into his lungs, where aspiration pneumonia can result.

Medicating a bird's food or offering medicated feed (such as tetracyline-laced pellets that were fed to imported birds during quarantine to prevent psittacosis) is another effective possibility. Medications added to a bird's water supply are often less effective because sick birds are less likely to drink water, and the medicated water may have an unusual taste that makes it even less appealing to the bird.

INJECTED MEDICATION

Avian veterinarians consider injections the most effective method of medicating birds. Some injection sites—into a vein, beneath the skin or into a bone—are used by avian veterinarians in the clinic. Bird owners are usually asked to medicate their birds intramuscularly, or by injecting medication into the bird's chest muscle. This is the area of the bird's body that

SIGNS OF ILLNESS

- a fluffed-up appearance
- a loss of appetite
- a desire to sleep all the time
- a change in the appearance or number of droppings
- weight loss
- listlessness
- drooping wings
- lameness
- partially eaten food stuck to the bird's face or food that has been regurgitated onto the cage floor
- labored breathing, with or without tail bobbing
- runny eyes or nose
- the bird stops talking or singing

If your bird shows any of these signs, please contact your veterinarian's office immediately for further instructions. Your bird should be seen as soon as possible to rule out any illnesses.

has the greatest muscle mass, so it is a good injection site. Ask the veterinarian to demonstrate giving an injection to your bird before you attempt to medicate him.

Once you are comfortable with the procedure, follow the veterinarian's instructions for injecting your bird. Wrap your bird securely, but comfortably, in a small towel, and lay him on your lap with his chest up. Hold his head securely with your thumb and index finger of one hand, and use the other to insert the syringe at about a 45° angle under the bird's chest feathers and into the muscle beneath.

You should remember to alternate the side of your bird you inject, to ensure that one side doesn't get overinjected and sore, and you should remain calm and talk to your bird in a soothing tone while you're administering the drugs. Before you both know it, the shot is over and your bird is one step closer to a complete recovery!

TOPICAL MEDICATION

Topical medication, which is far less stressful than an injection, provides medication directly to part of a bird's body. Uses can include medications for eye infections, dry skin on the feet or legs or sinus problems.

My parrot and I are living proof that all the methods described above work and are survivable by both bird and owner. She has received oral and injectable antibiotics for recurring infections, and she has had topical ointments applied to her feet to clear up a dry skin problem. Although I would have doubted that I would be able to give her injections when I first adopted her nine years ago, I now know that I can do it with a minimal amount of stress for both of us.

Conure Health Concerns

Conures are prone to feather picking (discussed in the next section of this book), papillomas and psittacine beak and feather disease syndrome. Conures fed seed-only diets can also become prone to vitamin A deficiency and other nutritionally related disorders.

When conures were being imported in large numbers, some of them were prone to a condition called Conure Bleeding Syndrome, which I will discuss briefly, although it does not appear with the frequency it did at the height of importation.

Conure Bleeding Syndrome

Conure Bleeding Syndrome has some symptoms in common with erythemic myelosis, which is a type of leukemia. The condition has been documented in Blue-crowns, Peach-fronts, Half moons and Patagonians. In Conure Bleeding Syndrome, affected birds suffer episodes of internal bleeding that eventually kill them. These birds will have nosebleeds, difficulty in breathing, weakness, diarrhea and excessive urination. The cause is unknown, but a lack of vitamin K, calcium and other minerals in a bird's diet may contribute to Conure Bleeding Syndrome. Other veterinary experts believe the condition is caused by a virus.

Papillomas

Papillomas are benign tumors that can appear almost anywhere on a bird's skin, including his foot, leg, eyelid or preen gland. If a bird has a papilloma on his cloaca, the bird may appear to have a "wet raspberry" coming out of his vent. These tumors, which are caused by a virus, can appear as small, crusty lesions, or they may be raised growths that have a bumpy texture or small projections.

Many papillomas can be left untreated without harm to the bird, but some must be removed by an avian veterinarian because a bird may pick at the growth and cause it to bleed.

Psittacine Beak and Feather Disease Syndrome

Psittacine Beak and Feather Disease Syndrome (PBFDS) is a virus that has been contracted in more than forty species of parrots, including conures. PBFDS causes a bird's feathers to become pinched or clubbed in appearance. Other symptoms include beak fractures and mouth ulcers. This highly contagious, fatal disease is most common in birds less than 3 years of age, and there is no cure at present.

FEATHER PICKING

Conure owners, particularly those who own Nandays and Suns, need to be on the alert for feather picking. Don't confuse picking with normal preening. Once feather picking begins, it may be difficult to get a bird to stop. Although it looks painful to us, some birds find the routine of pulling out their feathers emotionally soothing.

Conures that suddenly begin picking their feathers, especially those under the wings, may have an intestinal parasite called *giardia*. If you notice that your bird suddenly starts pulling his feathers out, contact your avian veterinarian for an evaluation. Other causes to consider include poor diet, low humidity, birds that are not allowed to bathe frequently and birds that do not have access to regular periods of light.

Psychological causes for feather picking can include boredom, insecurity, breeding frustrations, nervousness and stress. Stress in a bird's life can result from something as simple as a rearrangement of the living room furniture to issues as complicated as bringing a new child or pet into the home.

I don't have a magic solution to offer except to ask that you have your bird evaluated by your avian veterinarian if he starts to pick, and if the cause isn't physical, please be patient with your feather-picking parrot as you try to distract him away from his feathers.

Household Hazards

One of the reasons you chose a conure as a pet is because it's such a curious, active bird. This curiosity and activity can lead your pet into all sorts of mischief around your home, some of which can be harmful to your bird.

Nonetheless, you shouldn't keep your bird locked up in his cage all the time. On the contrary, all parrots need time out of their cages to maintain physical and mental health. The key to keeping your bird safe and healthy is to watch over him and play with him when he's out of his cage. Both of you will come to enjoy these playtimes greatly.

Some household hazards to be aware of (dangers to conures are included in parenthesis) include:

- unscreened windows and doors (escape potential)
- mirrors (collision and injury potential)
- exposed electrical cords (possible electrocution if chewed on)
- toxic houseplants (poisoning)
- unattended ashtrays (burns from lit cigarettes or poisoning from ingesting cigarette butts)
- venetian blind cords (hanging)
- sliding glass doors (open: escape potential/closed: collision and injury potential)
- ceiling fans (injury potential)
- open washing machines, dryers, refrigerators, freezers, ovens or dishwashers (bird flies into, is trapped and forgotten and dies when appliance is activated)
- open toilet bowls (drowning)
- uncovered fish tanks (drowning)
- leaded stained-glass items or inlaid jewelry (poisoning)
- uncovered cooking pots on the stove (drowning/scalding/poisoning/burns potential)
- crayons and permanent markers (poisoning)
- pesticides, rodent killers and snail bait (poisoning)
- untended stove burners (burns)
- candles (burns)
- open trash cans (injury by flying into and possibly being tossed out with the trash)

Parrot-proofing your home is akin to baby-proofing it. If you consider that the average macaw or cockatoo is intellectually and emotionally a perpetual 2 year old, you'll have some idea of the responsibility parrot owners take on when they adopt their pets. Although your conure is smaller than a cockatoo or a macaw, she is no less curious than her larger cousins and no less precious than larger birds are to their owners, so be aware of the potential dangers found in your home.

The dangers don't stop with the furniture and accessories. A plethora of fumes can overpower your conure, such as those from cigarettes, air fresheners, insecticides, bleach, shoe polish, oven cleaners, kerosene, lighter fluid, glues, active self-cleaning ovens, hair spray, overheated nonstick cookware, paint thinner, bathroom cleaners or nail polish remover. Try to keep your pet away from anything that has a strong chemical odor, and be sure to apply makeup and hair-care products far away from your conure.

To help protect your pet from harmful chemical fumes, consider using some "green" cleaning alternatives, such as baking soda and vinegar to clear clogged drains, baking soda instead of scouring powder to clean tubs and sinks, lemon juice and mineral oil to polish furniture, and white vinegar and water as a window cleaner. Not only will you help your conure stay healthy, you'll make the environment healthier, too!

Home remodeling and improvement projects can also cause harm to your conure. Fumes from paint or formaldehyde, which can be found in carpet backing, paneling and particle board, can cause pets and people to become ill. If you are having work done on your home, consider boarding your conure at your avian veterinarian's office or at the home of a bird-loving friend or relative until the project is complete and the house is aired out fully. You can consider the house safe for your pet when you cannot smell any trace of any of the products used in the remodeling.

Another potentially hazardous situation arises when you have your home fumigated for termites or other pests. Ask about treatments, such as electrical currents or liquid nitrogen, which harm the pests without harming your bird. If your house must be treated chemically, arrange to board your bird at your avian veterinarian's office or with a friend before, during and after the fumigation to ensure that no harm comes to your pet. Make sure your house is aired out completely before bringing your bird home.

If you have other pets in the home that require flea treatments, consider pyrethrin-based products. These natural flea killers are derived from chrysanthemums and, although they aren't as long-lasting as synthetic substitutes, they do knock down fleas quickly and are safer in the long run for your pets and you. Or you can treat your dog or cat's sleeping area with diatomaceous earth, which is the crushed shells of primitive one-celled algae. This dust kills fleas by mechanical means, which means that fleas will never develop a resistance to it as they could with chemical products.

Other pets can harm your conure's health, too. A curious cat could claw or bite your pet, a dog could step on him accidentally or bite him, or another bird could break his leg or rip off his upper mandible with his beak. If your conure tangles with another pet in your home, contact your avian veterinarian immediately, because emergency treatment (for bacterial infection from a puncture wound or shock from being stepped on or suffering a broken bone) may be required to save your bird's life.

PLANTS TO LOOK OUT FOR

Even common houseplants can pose a threat to your pet's health. Here are some plants that are considered **poisonous** to parrots:

- amaryllis
- calla lily
- daffodil
- dieffenbachia
- lily-of-the-valley
- mistletoe
- philodendron
- rhododendron

What's a conure owner to do? Are there any safe plants that you can keep in your home without endangering your feathered friend? Fortunately, yes, there are.

Some plants that are considered **safe** for pet birds include:

- African violets
- aloe
- coleus
- edible fig
- ferns
- gardenia
- grape ivy

Be sure that you don't treat any of these bird-safe plants with insecticides or chemical fertilizers.

Conure First Aid

Sometimes your bird will get himself into a situation that will require quick thinking and even quicker action on your part to help save him from serious injury or death. Make sure you have your bird owner's first-aid kit (see sidebar in this chapter for information on what to include).

ANIMAL BITES

Infections can develop from bacteria on the biting animal's teeth and/or claws. Also, a bird's internal organs can be damaged by the bite. Sometimes the bite marks can be seen, but often the bird shows few, if any, signs of injury.

Call your veterinarian's office and transport the bird there immediately. Treatment for shock and antibiotics is often the course of action veterinarians take to save birds that have been bitten.

BEAK INJURY

A bird needs both his upper and lower beak (also called the upper and lower mandible) to eat and preen properly. Infections can set in rather quickly if a beak is fractured or punctured.

An obvious symptom is that the bird is bleeding from his beak. This often occurs after the bird flies into a windowpane or mirror, or if he has a run-in with an operational ceiling fan. A bird may have also cracked or damaged his beak, and portions of the beak may be missing.

Control bleeding. Keep the bird calm and quiet. Contact your avian veterinarian's office.

BLEEDING

A bird can withstand about a 20 percent loss of blood volume and still recover from an injury. In the event of external bleeding, you will see blood on the bird, his cage and his surroundings. In the case of internal bleeding, the bird may pass bloody droppings or bleed from his nose, mouth or vent.

For external bleeding, apply direct pressure. If the bleeding doesn't stop with direct pressure, apply a coagulant, such as styptic powder (for nails and beaks) or cornstarch (for broken feathers and skin injuries). If the bleeding stops, observe the bird for a recurrence of the bleeding or for shock. Call your veterinarian's office if the bird seems weak or if he has lost a lot of blood.

In the case of broken blood feathers, you may have to remove the feather shaft to stop the bleeding. To do this, grasp the feather shaft as close to the skin as you can with a pair of needle-nosed pliers and pull out the shaft with a swift, steady motion. Apply direct pressure to the skin after you remove the feather shaft.

BREATHING PROBLEMS

Respiratory problems in pet birds can be life-threatening.

Symptoms include the bird wheezing or clicking while breathing, bobbing his tail, breathing with an open mouth, experiencing discharge from his nares or swelling around his eyes.

Keep the bird warm, place him in a bathroom with a hot shower running to help him breathe easier and call your veterinarian's office.

FIRST-AID KIT

Assemble a bird owner's first-aid kit so that you will have some basic supplies on hand before your bird needs them. Here's what to include:

- towels for catching and holding your bird

- a heating pad

- a pad of paper and pencil

- styptic powder or cornstarch to stop bleeding

- blunt-tipped scissors

- nail clippers and nail file

- needle-nosed pliers to pull broken blood feathers

- blunt-end tweezers

- hydrogen peroxide

- an eye irrigation solution

- bandage materials

- an eye dropper

- syringes to irrigate wounds or feed sick birds

- a penlight

BURNS

Birds that are burned severely enough can go into shock and may die. A burned bird has reddened skin and burnt or greasy feathers. The bird may also show signs of shock (see below for details).

Mist the burned area with cool water. Apply an antibiotic cream or spray lightly. **Do not apply any oily or greasy substances**, including butter. If the bird seems shocked or the burn is widespread, contact your veterinarian's office for further instructions.

CONCUSSION

A concussion results from a sharp blow to the head that can cause injury to the brain. Birds sometimes suffer concussions when they fly into mirrors or windows. They will seem stunned and may go into shock.

Keep the bird warm, prevent him from hurting himself further and watch him carefully. Alert your veterinarian's office to the injury.

CLOACAL PROLAPSE

In this situation, the bird's lower intestines, uterus or cloaca is protruding from the bird's vent. You will notice pink, red, brown or black tissue protruding from his vent.

Contact your veterinarian's office for immediate follow-up care. Your veterinarian can usually reposition the organs.

EGG BINDING

With egg binding, the egg blocks the hen's excretory system and makes it impossible for her to eliminate. Also, eggs can sometimes break inside the hen, which can lead to infection.

An egg-bound hen strains to lay eggs unsuccessfully. She becomes fluffed and lethargic, sits on the floor of her cage, may be paralyzed and may have a swollen abdomen.

Keep the hen warm, because this sometimes helps her pass the egg. Put her and her cage into a warm bathroom with a hot shower running to increase the humidity, which may also help her pass the egg. If your bird doesn't improve shortly (within an hour), contact your veterinarian.

Eye Injury

Untreated eye problems may lead to blindness. Symptoms include swollen or pasty eyelids, discharge, cloudy eyeballs and increased rubbing of eye area.

Examine the eye carefully for foreign bodies. Contact your veterinarian for more information.

Fracture

A fracture can cause a bird to go into shock. Depending on the type of fracture, infections can also set in.

Birds most often break bones in their legs, so be on the lookout for a bird that is holding one leg at an odd angle or that isn't putting weight on one leg. Sudden swelling of a leg or wing or a droopy wing can also indicate fractures.

Confine the bird to his cage or a small carrier. Don't handle him unnecessarily. Keep him warm and contact your veterinarian.

> **HEALTH TIP**
>
> Please don't kiss your conure on the beak (kiss him on top of his head instead) or allow your bird to put his head into your mouth, nibble on your lips or preen your teeth. Although you may see birds doing this on television or in pictures in a magazine and think that it's a cute trick, it's really unsafe for your bird's health and well-being.

Frostbite

A bird could lose toes or feet to frostbite. He could also go into shock and die as a result. The frostbitten area is very cold and dry to the touch and is pale in color.

Warm up the damaged tissue gradually in a circulating water bath. Keep the bird warm and contact your veterinarian's office for further instructions.

Inhaled or Eaten Foreign Object

Birds can develop serious respiratory or digestive problems from foreign objects in their bodies. Wheezing and other respiratory problems will result from an inhaled item. If you noticed that your bird was playing with a small item that suddenly cannot be found, he may have swallowed it.

If you suspect that your bird has inhaled or eaten something he shouldn't, contact your veterinarian's office immediately.

LEAD POISONING

Birds can die from lead poisoning. A bird with lead poisoning may act depressed or weak. He may go blind, or he may walk in circles at the bottom of his cage. He may regurgitate or pass droppings that resemble tomato juice.

Contact your avian veterinarian immediately. Lead poisoning requires a response for successful treatment, and the treatment may require several days or weeks to complete.

Note: Lead poisoning is easily prevented by keeping birds away from common sources of lead in the home. These include stained-glass items, leaded paint found in some older homes, fishing weights, drapery weights and parrot toys (some are weighted with lead).

OVERHEATING

High body temperatures can kill a bird. An overheated bird will try to make himself "thin." He will hold his wings away from his body, open his mouth and roll his tongue in an attempt to cool himself. Birds don't have sweat glands, so they must try to cool their bodies by exposing as much of their skin's surface as they can to moving air. Cool the bird off by putting him in front of a fan (make sure the blades are screened so the bird doesn't injure himself further), by spraying him with cool water or by having him stand in a bowl of cool water. Let the bird drink cool water if he can (if he can't, offer him cool water with an eyedropper) and contact your veterinarian.

POISONING

Poisons can kill a bird quickly. Poisoned birds may suddenly regurgitate, have diarrhea or bloody droppings and have redness or burns around their mouths. They may also go into convulsions, become paralyzed or go into shock. Put the poison out of your bird's reach. Contact your veterinarian for further instructions. Be prepared to take the poison with you to the vet's office in case he or she needs to contact a poison control center for further information.

SEIZURES

Seizures can indicate a number of serious conditions, including lead poisoning, infections, nutritional deficiency, heatstroke and epilepsy. The bird goes into a seizure that lasts from a few seconds to a minute. Afterward, he seems dazed and may stay on the cage floor for several hours. He may also appear unsteady and won't perch.

Keep the bird from hurting himself further by removing everything you can from his cage. Cover the bird's cage with a towel and darken the room to reduce the bird's stress level. Contact your veterinarian's office for further instructions immediately.

SHOCK

Shock indicates that the bird's circulatory system cannot move the blood supply around the bird's body. This is a serious condition that can lead to death if left untreated.

Shocked birds may act depressed, they may breathe rapidly and they may have a fluffed appearance. If your bird displays any of these signs in conjunction with a recent accident, suspect shock and take appropriate action.

Keep your bird warm, cover his cage and transport him to your veterinarian's office as soon as possible.

URGENT CARE ADVICE

In *The Complete Bird Owner's Handbook*, veterinarian Gary Gallerstein offers the following "don'ts" to bird owners whose birds need urgent care:

- Don't give a bird human medications or medications prescribed for another animal unless so directed by your veterinarian.

- Don't give your bird medications that are suggested by a friend, a store employee or even a human physician.

- Don't give a bird alcohol or laxatives.

- Don't apply any oils or ointments to your bird unless your veterinarian tells you to do so.

- Don't bathe a sick bird.

Emergency Tips

Veterinarian Michael Murray recommends that bird owners keep the following tips in mind when facing emergency situations:

Keep the bird warm. You can do this by putting the bird in an empty aquarium with a heating pad under him, by putting a heat lamp near the bird's cage or by putting a heating pad set on low under the bird's cage in place of the cage tray. Whatever heat source you choose to use, make sure to keep a close eye on your bird so that he doesn't accidentally burn himself on the pad or lamp or that he doesn't chew on a power cord.

Put the bird in a dark, quiet room. This helps reduce the bird's stress.

Put the bird's food in locations that are easy to reach. Sick birds need to eat, but they may not be able to reach food in its normal locations in the cage. Sometimes, birds require hand-feeding to keep their calorie consumption steady.

Protect the bird from additional injury. If the convalescing bird is in a clear-sided aquarium, for example, you may want to put a towel over the glass to keep the bird from flying into it.

When Your Conure Dies

Although conures are relatively long-lived pets, eventually the wonderful relationship between bird and owner ends when the bird dies. While no one has an easy time accepting the death of a beloved pet, children may have more difficulty with the loss than adults. To help your child cope, consider the following suggestions:

Let your child know that it's okay to feel sad about losing your conure. Encourage your child to draw pictures of the bird, to make a collage using photos of your pet or pictures of conures from magazines, to write stories or poems about him or to talk about the loss. Also explain to the child that these sad feelings will pass with time. Regardless of a child's age, being honest about the loss of your bird is the best approach to help all family members cope with the loss.

While helping their children cope with the death of a pet, parents need to remember that it's okay for adults to feel sad, too. Don't diminish your feelings of loss by saying "It's only a bird." Pets fill important roles in our lives and our families. Whenever we lose someone close to us, we grieve.

If someone in your family needs to discuss the loss further, the University of California has established a pet-loss support hot line. Call 916/752-4200 for further information. The Delta Society also maintains a directory of pet-loss resources. More information about this

You will always have memories of the great times you've had with your conure.

directory is available by calling 206/226-7357. Your avian veterinarian's office may know of pet-loss support groups in your area, or you may be able to find one by contacting a local animal shelter or SPCA office. Finally, some pet-loss support groups are available on-line through the Internet.

Although you may feel as though you never want another bird because of the pain caused by your bird's death, don't let the loss of your conure keep you from owning other birds. While you can never replace your conure completely, you may find that you miss having a feathered companion around your house. Some people will want a new pet bird almost immediately after suffering a loss, while others will want to wait a few weeks or months before bringing another bird home. Maybe you want another conure, or perhaps you'd like to try owning a different avian species. Discuss bringing home a new pet bird with your family, your avian veterinarian and bird breeders in your area. Together, I'm sure you can work out a plan that's best for you!

Enjoying
Your

part three

Conure

Your
Conure's
Behavior

The following common avian behaviors are listed in alphabetical order to help you better understand your new feathered friend!

ATTENTION-GETTING BEHAVIORS

As your conure becomes more settled in your home, don't be surprised if you hear subtle little fluffs coming from under the cage cover first thing in the morning. It's as if your bird is saying, "I hear that you're up. I'm up, too. Don't forget to uncover me and play with me!" Other attention-getting behaviors include gently shaking toys, sneezing or soft vocalizations.

BATHING

Conures are great bathers that love to be dunked under the water faucet while sitting on their owner's hand or to stand under a light shower in the kitchen sink. Some birds may even enjoy showering with their owners, and bird-sized shower perches can be purchased or made if you want your bird to shower

Conures love light showers in the sink and bird-sized baths.

with you. If nothing else is available, your conure will try to take a bath in her water bowl. Be sure your pet's bath water is lukewarm before letting your conure take a quick dip, and allow plenty of time for your bird's feathers to dry before she goes to bed to avoid chilling your pet.

BEAK GRINDING

If you hear your bird making odd little grinding noises as she's drifting off to sleep, don't be alarmed! Beak grinding is a sign of a contented pet bird, and it's commonly heard as a bird settles in for the night.

BEAK WIPING

After a meal, it's common for a conure to wipe her beak against a perch, on your sleeve (if your arm happens to be handy) or on the cage bars to clean it.

BIRDIE AEROBICS

This is how I describe a sudden bout of stretching that all parrots seem prone to. An otherwise calm bird will suddenly grab the cage bars and stretch the wing and leg muscles on one side of her body, or she will raise both wings in imitation of an eagle. Again, this is normal behavior.

BITING

If your conure bites you in the presence of strangers, she is demonstrating an instinctive flock behavior. In the wild, when conures are presented with a threat (such as the stranger), they call to one another to flee, and then even bite at slower-moving members of the flock to hurry them on their way.

If your bird bites you when you are alone, she may simply be testing her environment with her mouth (see "tasting/testing") or she may be demonstrating how well she has trained you! If you react with a lot of dramatic attention (such as using a loud voice or shaking your finger at the bird), the bird will think she has stumbled onto a great game that you will play with her each time she bites you.

Finally, a biting bird may be challenging you for control of her environment. If you want to maintain control of your bird and her environment, look sternly at your pet and use the "Up" command (described in the "Taming Your Conure" section of this chapter) to get the bird on your hand. This should help keep the biting episodes to a minimum.

It is perfectly normal for an otherwise healthy conure to take short naps during the day.

CATNAPS

Don't be surprised if you catch your conure taking a little catnap during the day. As long as you see no other indications of illness, such as a loss of appetite or a fluffed-up appearance, there is no need to worry if your pet sleeps during the day.

CHEWING

Chewing helps keep a pet bird's beak in top condition, and it also provides a pet parrot with a way to use up some of her excess energy. Chewing is one of a conure's most common behaviors, which means your pet will need an abundant supply of chewable toys. These can range from empty paper towel rolls to elaborate wooden toys you purchase at the pet store. If you don't provide a conure with proper outlets for her chewing urges, she will find satisfaction in gnawing on your furniture or houseplants. Be sure to supervise your conure when she is out of her cage to prevent her from chewing on inappropriate and potentially harmful things in your home.

Eye Pinning

When a conure sees something that really excites or interests her, you may notice that her pupils contract, expand and contract again. This is called eye pinning. This action will be easier to see on some conures than on others because some conure species have dark irises that blend in quite well with their pupils.

Fluffing

Fluffing is often a prelude to preening or a tension releaser. If your bird fluffs up, stays fluffed and resembles a feathered pine cone, however, contact your avian veterinarian for an appointment because fluffed feathers can be an indicator of illness.

Conures preen each other as a sign of great affection.

Mutual Preening

This is part of the preening behavior described below, and it can take place between birds or between birds and their owners. It is a sign of affection reserved for

111

best friends or mates, so consider it an honor if your conure wants to preen your eyebrows, hair, mustache or beard, or your arms and hands. If your conure wants to be preened, she will approach you with her head down and will gently nudge her head under your hand as if to tell you exactly where she wants to be scratched and petted.

PAIR BONDING

Not only do mated pairs bond, but best bird buddies of the same sex will demonstrate some of the same behavior, including sitting close to each other, preening each other and mimicking the other's actions, such as stretching or scratching, often at the same time.

POSSESSIVENESS

Although it doesn't happen as often with conures as with some other parrot species, a conure can become overly attached to one person in the household, especially if that same person is the one who is primarily responsible for her care. Indications of a possessive conure can include biting and other threatening gestures made toward other family members, and pair bonding behavior with the chosen family member.

You can keep your conure from becoming possessive by having all members of the family spend time with your bird from the time you first bring her home. Encourage different members of the family to feed the bird and clean her cage, and make sure all family members play with the bird and socialize with her while she's out of her cage.

FEATHERED WARNINGS

Your conure's feathers are one of the most fascinating organs of her body. The bird uses feathers for movement, warmth and balance, among other things. The following are some feather-related behaviors that can indicate health problems for your conure.

Fluffing: A healthy conure will fluff before preening or for short periods. If your conure seems to remain fluffed up for an extended period, see your avian veterinarian. This can be a sign of illness in birds.

Mutual Preening: Two birds will preen each other affectionately, but if you notice excessive feather loss, make sure one bird is not picking on the other and pulling out healthy feathers.

Feather Picking: A healthy bird will preen often to keep her feathers in top shape. However, a bird under stress may start to preen excessively and severe feather loss can result.

PREENING

This is part of a conure's normal routine. You will see your bird ruffling and straightening her feathers each day. She will also take oil from the uropygial or preen gland at the base of her tail and put the oil on the rest of her feathers, so don't be concerned if you see your pet seeming to peck or bite at her tail. If, during molting, your bird seems to remove whole feathers, don't panic! Old, worn feathers are pushed out by incoming new ones, which makes the old feathers loose and easy to remove.

When your conure is preening, she is spreading natural oil from a gland at the base of her tail onto her other feathers.

REGURGITATING

If you see that your bird is pinning her eyes, bobbing her head and pumping her neck and crop muscles, she is about to regurgitate some food for you. Birds regurgitate to their mates during breeding season and to their young while raising chicks. It is a mark of great affection, so try not to be too disgusted if your pet starts bringing up her last meal in your honor.

RESTING ON ONE FOOT

Do not be alarmed if you see your conure occasionally resting on only one foot. This is normal behavior (the resting foot is often drawn up into the belly feathers). If you see your bird always using both feet to perch, please contact your avian veterinarian because this can indicate a health problem.

113

SCREAMING

Well-cared-for conures will vocalize, but birds that feel neglected and that have little attention paid to them may become screamers. Once a bird becomes a screamer, it can be a difficult habit to break, particularly because the bird feels rewarded by your negative attention every time she screams. You may not see your attention as a reward, but at least the bird gets to see you and to hear from you as you tell her to be quiet.

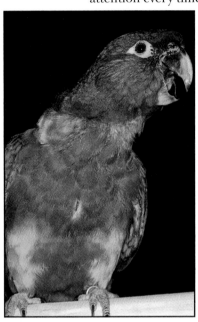

If your bird screams, try calling to her with a reassuring voice to let her know you are there.

Sometimes, conures and other parrots are just a little lonesome and in need of reassurance, so they scream to see where their people are. In these cases, simply call back to your bird with a "I'm here. Are you okay?" or another reassuring phrase. In many cases, the bird will quiet down quickly after hearing your voice.

At other times, birds may scream because something in the environment frightens them. In these cases, you will have to work with the bird over time to desensitize her to whatever is scary. If your bird screams at you when you wear a hat, for example, set the hat on a table far away from the bird's cage and gradually (over a period of a few days or a week), bring the hat closer to your bird's cage. Tell your bird how brave she is as the hat gets closer to the cage, and cuddle her and pet her to further reward her bravery.

Still other birds scream because they think they have to "protect" their home and families. This hearkens back to the wild, where parrots alert each other to danger in the area by screaming or calling to one another. In these cases, it's a good idea to check to see that your toaster isn't smoking or there isn't a squirrel on the patio railing before disciplining your helpful watch-parrot.

Sometimes birds will scream when they are tired. In these cases, covering the cage for a few minutes does the trick. If your bird seems to be consistently tired and cranky, you may have to adjust her bedtime. Remember that birds need about twelve hours of sleep a night, and your bird may be disturbed by evening activities, such as the family watching TV or the children doing homework with a bright desk lamp on. A heavier cage cover or relocating the bird to another part of the house should do the trick in these cases, but remember not to banish your bird to some far-flung, seldom-used part of your house because this can also cause screaming if the bird feels neglected and forgotten.

Remember to give your bird consistent attention (at least two hours a day); provide her with an interesting environment, complete with a variety of toys and a well-balanced diet and leave a radio or television on when you're away to provide background noise, and your bird shouldn't become a screamer.

SLEEPING

Conures are known for two unusual behaviors while sleeping: snuggling under something to sleep and falling asleep on their backs in their food bowls. You may find your bird napping under a corner of her cage paper (if the cage she lives in doesn't have a grille to keep the bird out of the cage tray). To keep your pet content, give your conure a washcloth, a fuzzy toy or something else cuddly to snuggle with.

Conures sometimes fall asleep in their food bowls or on the cage floor on their backs with their feet in the air. Although this position has an alarming effect on new conure owners, there's nothing wrong with your pet. This is a perfectly comfortable position for a conure to be in.

SNEEZING

In pet birds, sneezes are classified as either nonproductive or productive. Nonproductive sneezes clear a bird's nares (what we think of as nostrils) and are nothing to worry about. Some birds even stick a claw into their nares to induce a sneeze from time to time, much as a snuff dipper used to take a pinch to produce the same effect. Productive sneezes, on the other hand, produce a discharge and are a cause for concern. If your bird sneezes frequently and you see a discharge from her nares or notice the area around her nares is wet, contact your avian veterinarian immediately to set up an appointment to have your bird's health checked.

Don't be alarmed if your conure wants to sleep or snuggle on her back—it's a normal behavior.

STRESS

Stress can show itself in many ways in your bird's behavior, including shaking, diarrhea, rapid breathing, wing and tail fanning, screaming, feather picking, poor sleeping habits or loss of appetite.

Over a period of time, stress can harm your conure's health. To prevent your bird from becoming stressed, try to provide her with as normal and regular a routine as possible. Parrots are, for the most part, creatures of habit, and they don't always adapt well to sudden changes in their environment or schedule. But if you do have to change something, talk to your parrot about it first. It may seem crazy, but telling your bird what you're going to do before you do it may actually help reduce her stress.

TASTING/TESTING THINGS

Birds use their beaks and mouths to explore their world in much the same way people use their hands. For example, don't be surprised if your conure reaches out to tentatively taste or bite your hand before stepping onto it for the first time. Your bird isn't biting you to be mean; she's merely investigating her world and testing the strength of a new perch using the tools she has available.

VOCALIZATION

Many parrots vocalize around sunrise and sunset, which may be a holdover from flock behavior in the wild. The parrots in the flock call to each other to start and end their days. You may notice that your pet conure calls to you when you are out of the room. This may mean that she feels lonely or that she needs some reassurance from you. Tell her that she's fine and that she's being a good bird, and the bird should settle down and begin playing or eating. If she continues to call to you, however, you may want to check on her to ensure that everything is all right.

YAWNING

You may notice your conure yawning from time to time or seeming to want to pop her ears by opening her mouth wide and closing it. Some bird experts would say your bird needs more oxygen in her environment and would recommend airing out your bird room (be sure all your window and door screens are secure before opening a window or sliding glass door to let fresh air in), while other experts would tell you your pet is merely yawning or stretching her muscles. If you see no other signs of illness, such as forceful regurgitation or vomiting, accompanying the yawning, you have no cause for concern.

Taming Your Conure

Before you can begin to handle your conure, you must first earn her trust. A good first step in building trust with your conure is getting her to become comfortable around you. To do this, give your bird a bit of warning before you approach her cage. Call her name when you walk into the room. Move slowly around your pet to help her become more comfortable with you. Reassure the bird that everything is all right and that she's a wonderful pet.

TAKING YOUR CONURE OUT OF HER CAGE

After your bird is comfortable having you in the same room with her, try placing your hand in her cage as a first step toward taking her out of her cage. Place your hand in your bird's cage and hold it there for a few seconds. Don't be surprised if your bird flutters around and squawks at first at the "intruder."

Continue this process daily, and leave your hand in the cage for slightly longer periods of time each day. Within a few days, your bird won't make a fuss about your hand being in her space, and she may come over to investigate this new perch. Do not remove your hand from the cage the first time your conure lands on it; just let the bird become accustomed to perching on your hand.

After several successful perching attempts on successive days, try to take your hand out of the cage with your bird on it. Some conures will take to this new adventure willingly, while others are reluctant to leave the safety and security of home. (Be sure your bird's wings are clipped and all doors and windows are secured before taking your bird out of her cage.)

It may take several days before your bird will be comfortable enough to perch on your hand.

TEACHING THE "STEP UP"

Once your conure is willing to come out of her cage on your hand, see if you can make perching on your hand a game for your pet. Once she masters perching on your hand, you can teach her to step up by gently pressing your finger up and into the bird's belly. This will cause the bird to step up. As she does so, say "Step up" or "Up." Before long, your bird will respond to this command without much prompting.

Along with the "Up" command, you may want to teach your conure the "Down" command. When you put the bird down on her cage or play gym, simply say "Down" as the bird steps off your hand. These two simple commands offer a great deal of control for you over your bird, because you can say "Up" to put an unruly bird back in her cage or you can tell a parrot that needs to go to bed "Down" as you put the bird in her cage at night.

After your bird has mastered the "Up" and "Down" commands, encourage her to climb a "ladder" by moving her from index finger to index finger (the "rungs"). Keep taming sessions short (about fifteen minutes is the maximum conure attention span) and make the taming process fun because it will be much more enjoyable for both of you.

Petting Your Conure

After your pet has become comfortable sitting on your hand, try petting her. Birds seem to like to have their heads, backs, cheek patches, underwing areas and eye areas (including the closed eyelids) scratched or petted lightly. Quite a few like to have a spot low on their backs at the bases of their tails (over their preen glands) rubbed. You'll have to experiment to see where your bird likes to be petted. You'll know you're successful if your bird clicks or grinds her beak, pins her eyes or settles onto your hand or into your lap with a completely relaxed, blissful expression on her face.

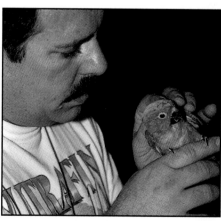

Conures usually like to have their heads, backs and cheek patches scratched lightly.

119

MISBEHAVIN'

From time to time, your conure will misbehave and need to be disciplined. When disciplining your conure, remember that parrots are not "cause and effect" thinkers. If your bird chews on the molding under the cabinets in your home office, she won't associate you yelling at her or locking her in her cage with the original misbehavior. As a result, most traditional forms of discipline are ineffective with parrots. You must especially be sure not to lose your temper with your bird and never to hit her, even if the bird makes you very angry.

So what do you do when your conure misbehaves? When you must discipline your pet, look at her sternly and tell her "No" in a firm voice. If the bird is climbing on or chewing something she shouldn't, also remove her from the source of danger and temptation as you tell her "No." If your bird has wound herself up into a screaming banshee, sometimes a little "time out" in her covered cage (between five and ten minutes in most cases) does wonders to calm her down. Once the screaming stops and the bird calms down enough to play quietly, eat or simply move around her cage, the cover comes off to reveal a well-behaved, calmed-down pet. In other cases, your screaming pet may just need to be reassured and held for a few minutes. With time and experience, you will soon be able to determine which types of screams require which type of response from you.

If your conure bites you while she's perched on your hand or if she begins chewing on your clothing or jewelry, you can often dissuade her from this behavior by rotating your wrist about a quarter-turn to simulate a small "earthquake." Your bird will quickly associate the rocking of her "perch" with her misbehavior and will stop biting or chewing.

TOILET TRAINING

Although some people don't believe it, conures and other parrots can be toilet trained so that they don't defecate on their owners. If you want to toilet train your bird, you will have to choose a word that will indicate the act of defecating to your pet, such as "Go poop" or "Go potty." While you're training your pet to associate the chosen phrase with the action when you see her about to defecate in her cage or on her play gym, you will have to train yourself to your bird's body language and actions that indicate she is about to defecate, such as shifting around or squatting slightly.

Once your bird seems to associate "Go potty" with defecating, you can try picking her up and holding her until she starts to shift or squat. Tell the bird to "Go potty" while placing her on her cage, where she can defecate. Once she's done, pick her up again and praise her for being such a smart bird! Expect a few accidents while you are both learning this trick, and soon you'll have a toilet-trained bird that you can put on her cage about every twenty minutes or so, give the command to and expect to defecate.

part four

Beyond the Basics

chapter 10

Resources

For more information on bird care, look for these books at your local library, bookstore or pet store:

Recommended Reading

ABOUT HEALTH CARE

Doane, Bonnie Munro. *The Parrot in Health and Illness: An Owner's Guide.* New York: Howell Book House, 1991.

Gallerstein, Gary A. DVM. *The Complete Bird Owner's Handbook.* New York: Howell Book House, 1994.

Ritchie, Branson W. DVM, PhD, Greg J. Harrison, DVM and Linda R. Harrison. *Avian Medicine: Principles and Application.* Lake Worth, Fla.: Wingers Publishing Inc., 1994.

ABOUT BREEDING

Gonzalez, Fran. *Breeding Exotic Birds: A Beginner's Guide.* Cypress, Calif.: Neon Pet Publications. 1993.

Schubot, Richard, Susan Clubb, DVM and Kevin Clubb. *Psittacine Aviculture.* Loxahatchee, Fla.: Avicultural Breeding and Research Center, 1992.

ABOUT TRAINING

Athan, Mattie Sue. *Guide to a Well-Behaved Parrot.* Hauppauge, N.Y.: Barron's Educational Series Inc., 1993.

Doane, Bonnie Munro and Thomas Qualkinbush. *My Parrot, My Friend.* New York: Howell Book House, 1994.

Hubbard, Jennifer. *The New Parrot Training Handbook.* Fremont, Cal.: Parrot Press, 1997.

ABOUT PET LOSS

Sife, Wallace PhD. *The New Revised Loss of a Pet.* New York: Howell Book House, 1998.

GENERAL TITLES

Alderton, David. *You and Your Pet Bird.* New York: Alfred A. Knopf, 1994.

Alderton, David. *A Birdkeeper's Guide to Pet Birds.* Blacksburg, Va.: Tetra Press, 1987.

Coborn, John. *The Professional's Book of Conures.* Neptune, N.J.: TFH Publications Inc., 1991.

Forshaw, Joseph. *Parrots of the World.* Neptune, N.J.: TFH Publications Inc., 1977.

Freud, Arthur. *The Parrot: An Owner's Guide to a Happy, Healthy Pet.* New York: Howell Book House, 1996.

The Duke of Bedford. *Parrots and Parrot-like Birds.* Neptune, N.J.: TFH Publications Inc., 1969 (U.S. distribution).

Vriends, Matthew. *Conures: A Complete Pet Owner's Manual.* Hauppauge, N.Y.: Barron's Educational Series Inc., 1992.

MAGAZINES

Bird Talk. 2401 Beverly Blvd., P.O. Box 57900, Los Angeles, CA 90057.

Birds USA. Look for it in your local bookstore or pet store.

Caged Bird Hobbyist. 7-L Dundas Circle, Greensboro, NC 27407.

On-line Resources

Bird-specific sites have been cropping up regularly on the Internet. These sites offer pet-bird owners the opportunity to share stories about their pets, as well as trade helpful hints about bird care.

If you belong to an on-line service, look for the pet site (it's sometimes included in more general topics, such as "Hobbies and Interests," or more specifically "Pets"). If you have Internet access, ask your Web Browser software to search for "conures," "parrots" or "pet birds."

Videos

The Positive Approach to Parrots as Pets: Understanding Bird Behavior (tape 1) and *Training Through Positive Reinforcement* (tape 2). Natural Encounters Inc., P.O. Box 68666, Indianapolis, IN 46268.

Bird Clubs

The American Federation of Aviculture
P.O. Box 56218
Phoenix, AZ 85079-6128

Avicultural Society of America
P.O. Box 5516
Riverside, CA 92517-5517

International Avicultural Society
P.O. Box 280383
Memphis, TN 38168

National Cage Bird Show Club, Inc.
25 Janss Rd.
Thousand Oaks, CA 91360

National Parrot Association
8 N. Hoffman Lane
Hauppage, NY 11788

Society of Parrot Breeders and Exhibitors
P.O. Box 369
Groton, MA 01450

Other Organizations

National Animal Poison Control Center Hot Line
(800) 548-2423

Parrot Rehabilitation Society
P.O. Box 6202213
San Diego, CA 92612

On-line Resources

Bird-specific sites have been cropping up regularly on the Internet. These sites offer pet-bird owners the opportunity to share stories about their pets, as well as trade helpful hints about bird care.

If you belong to an on-line service, look for the pet site (it's sometimes included in more general topics, such as "Hobbies and Interests," or more specifically "Pets"). If you have Internet access, ask your Web Browser software to search for "conures," "parrots" or "pet birds."

Videos

The Positive Approach to Parrots as Pets: Understanding Bird Behavior (tape 1) and *Training Through Positive Reinforcement* (tape 2). Natural Encounters Inc., P.O. Box 68666, Indianapolis, IN 46268.

Bird Clubs

The American Federation of Aviculture
P.O. Box 56218
Phoenix, AZ 85079-6128

Avicultural Society of America
P.O. Box 5516
Riverside, CA 92517-5517

International Avicultural Society
P.O. Box 280383
Memphis, TN 38168

National Cage Bird Show Club, Inc.
25 Janss Rd.
Thousand Oaks, CA 91360

National Parrot Association
8 N. Hoffman Lane
Hauppage, NY 11788

Society of Parrot Breeders and Exhibitors
P.O. Box 369
Groton, MA 01450

Other Organizations

National Animal Poison Control Center Hot Line
(800) 548-2423

Parrot Rehabilitation Society
P.O. Box 6202213
San Diego, CA 92612